Dear Reader,

The book you are holding is one of the books from the IIMA Business Books series published in collaboration with Random House to disseminate knowledge to executives in a manner that brings them up to date in different fields of management. The books are written by authors who have rich experience of teaching executives from a diverse set of organizations. Written in a conversational style with numerous illustrations from the world of experience, you will find the books useful in your work life. The references cited in the books provide you with ready information on where to look for more detailed information on specific topics and concepts. I am certain you will enjoy reading the book. Write to us suggesting topics that you will like being covered in the books that are to be published under the series in the future.

Samir K. Barua
Director
IIM Ahmedabad

100

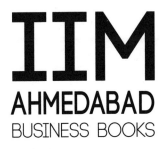

Strategies for Success

THE PERSUASIVE MANAGER
Communication Strategies for 21st Century Managers

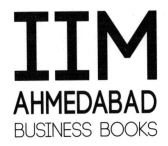

IIM
AHMEDABAD
BUSINESS BOOKS

Strategies for Success

THE PERSUASIVE MANAGER
Communication Strategies for 21st Century Managers

M.M. MONIPPALLY

RANDOM HOUSE INDIA

First published by Random House India in 2010
Ninth impression in 2014

Random House Publishers India Private Limited
Windsor IT Park, 7th Floor, Tower-B
A-1, Sector-125, Noida-201301, UP

Random House Group Limited
20 Vauxhall Bridge Road
London SW1V 2SA
United Kingdom

978 81 8400 149 5

Typeset in Cronos Pro by InoSoft Systems, Noida

Printed and bound in India by Replika Press Pvt. Ltd.

For Philo:
My friend. My wife.

A Word or Two Before You Start...

If you are looking for the latest techniques that will help you sell anything to anyone in fifty-nine seconds or less, you've picked up a wrong book. It has no quick fixes to offer. Please put it back on the shelf and continue your search. I wish you good luck.

If you are looking for a jargon-free book that will help you review systematically your multiple managerial relationships—with your bosses, peers, subordinates, vendors, and customers—and enhance your persuasiveness, you've picked up the right book. Read on. And reflect.

You need to figure out what kind of persuasion suits your personality, your strengths, your weaknesses, and environment. You need to identify the kind of people you can persuade easily and the kind of people you have difficulty persuading. You need to review your successes and find out why you succeed. Similarly, you need to review your failures and find out why you fail. Only then will you be able to repeat successes and prevent failures with some measure of confidence. You also need to identify the environment in which others persuade you easily, perhaps fraudulently, so that you can resist it. This book will give you the basic tools and examples to help you perform that analysis systematically and become more persuasive in your communication.

Persuasion is not the monopoly of a few professional persuaders such as advertisers and marketers. It is in everyone's blood. Yet we never reach the stage where we can say there's nothing more to learn. We can learn from one another irrespective of our age, profession, length of managerial experience, and position in the organizational hierarchy. That is why I have included in the book real-life accounts by managers working at different levels in a variety of organizations and facing different kinds of persuasion challenges.

I will be delighted to receive your feedback on this book. If you have any suggestions to improve any aspect of this book or if you have an interesting experience as a persuader or persuadee that you would like to share with readers, please get in touch with me (mpally@iimahd.ernet.in). I will be happy to include your persuasion experiences either on the book's website (www.iimabooks.com) or in the next edition of this book. Readers will then be invited to analyse those accounts and help everyone see why they worked or why they failed.

Similarly, I will be grateful if you let me know of any great persuaders you have come across in your own organization or elsewhere. We will all benefit if we study them and share their secrets with the rest of the world.

You are invited to visit and contribute to my blog (www.PersuasiveManager.blogspot.com). It is a collective exploration of management by persuasion. Several current events and issues are analysed regularly from the perspective of persuasion. Additional resources that will help you become more persuasive have also been introduced.

Thank you!

Naushad Noorani of ACC Ltd put me in touch with some of the remarkably persuasive managers whose accounts have been incorporated in this book.

Several Indian managers working in India and abroad shared with me their insights into persuasion by narrating the way they faced the challenge of persuasion.

Aman Narang, student of Institute of Technology, Banaras Hindu University, helped me with library research.

Colleagues Smeeta Mishra, Divya Poduval, and Pooja Susan Thomas went through the manuscript and gave me many helpful suggestions.

Anirban Sarma, Chiki Sarkar, and Priyanka Sarkar of Random House India also read the manuscript critically and refined the text.

I would like to thank all of you for your invaluable contribution to *The Persuasive Manager*.

CONTENTS

Introduction   xiii

1. It Pays to be a Persuasive Manager   1

2. The Basics of Persuasion   21

3. The Persuasive Boss   50

4. The Persuasive Subordinate   73

5. The Persuasive Peer   97

6. The Persuasive Vendor   124

7. The Persuasive Speaker   149

8. The Persuasive Writer   177

9. The Ethical Persuader   200

10. The Resistant Persuadee   225

11. Conclusion   255

Introduction

If you have a four-year old at home, you don't need to step out or read any books to learn about persuasion. All you need to do is observe her. She knows little about the world. She has no money. She is so tiny that adults around must look like giants to her. In spite of all these handicaps, she manages to have her way most of the time. She melts most parental resistance. What is her secret?

She cries. She smiles. At times she throws a tantrum. She refuses to walk or to be carried. She plonks down in the middle of the road and embarrasses her parents in public. She figures out early on what works with whom. She knows when to appeal to Daddy and when to involve *Dadi*. She realizes the enormous power she holds over adults, especially her parents and grandparents. She may not figure out why, but she discovers early on that even something as simple as refusing to eat will bring those grown-ups to their knees.

If we recall our own childhood, we will find that we also went through this glorious stage. We got our parents and elders to do our bidding. Are we all born persuaders then? We may or may not be. But right from the early weeks of life, we unconsciously employed many techniques of persuasion and enjoyed the fruits of its power.

We also learned the limitations of that power when we stepped out of home and started school. Many techniques that worked like magic at home didn't work on teachers, classmates, or on other adults. Some of us figured out why, adapted ourselves accordingly, revised our techniques, and continued to enjoy the power of persuasion in different contexts. Some of us lagged behind with our ability to persuade restricted to a few people in a few contexts. As managers, however, we have to deal with many kinds of people at different levels within the organization and outside.

There are three kinds of managers, according to a team of influence researchers led by David Kipnis (1984): shotgun managers, tacticians, and bystanders. Shotgun managers use influence tactics indiscriminately in order to get what they want. They are not particularly successful. Tacticians choose their influence strategies carefully and are generally successful. They occupy positions of power largely through their knowledge and skills. Bystander managers have little or no influence on their organizations. Not surprisingly, few of their objectives are achieved.

We must become tacticians and enhance our persuasive power in all directions–upward, downward, and horizontal–if we want to succeed as managers and if we want our organizations to prosper. The only way to pluck the high-hanging fruit is to stand on other people's shoulders. Unless they are willing shoulders, we should expect them to shake us down anytime.

Persuasion is by no means a new bag of tricks. It is as old as humanity. It started growing around the time hunter-gatherers realized that there were smarter ways than brute force to find food, shelter, and mates. Ancient scriptures and mythologies are full of stories that illustrate the use of sophisticated persuasion techniques by men and women, by gods and goddesses. Even the study of persuasion is centuries old. Aristotle's ideas on persuasion captured in *The Rhetoric* have had an enormous influence on the way persuasion is understood even today.

Many scholars have studied the multiple faces of persuasion and underlying forces, especially during the last few decades. They have produced a rich collection of both academic papers and popular books. There is little strikingly original that anyone can say about persuasion any more. The objective of this book, therefore, is to bring to you, in an accessible form, insights from many scholars of organizational power, influence, and persuasion that will help you

▶ systematically analyse your experience of persuasion at the workplace
▶ identify your strengths and weaknesses as a persuader in your multiple roles
▶ develop a framework for ethical persuasion
▶ plan your persuasion attempts strategically, and
▶ guard against being persuaded deceptively.

This book is divided into three parts. The first part, consisting of Chapters 1 and 2, forms the basis of the entire book. It gives you a concise account of the principles and techniques of persuasion. The second part, which consists of Chapters 3 to 8, deals with specific persuasion challenges relating to your subordinates, peers, bosses, and customers. It also deals with the challenges involved in oral persuasion and written persuasion. The third and final part consists of two chapters. Chapter 9 explores ethical persuasion while Chapter 10 focuses on how to resist persuasion, especially when the persuader uses deceptive means. The book ends with a short concluding section that shows how to take the learning forward.

The techniques and strategies of persuasion discussed in the book are illustrated with short, real-life cases mainly from the corporate world, both Indian and international. There are significant similarities between the strategies adopted by persuaders across different cultures and geographic locations. Therefore, this book has lessons for managers of all descriptions. The most important of them, however, is that we should aim to become persuasive managers rather than masters of persuasion techniques.

While different chapters are reasonably independent of one another, it is best to start with the first two chapters and then go to any chapter that interests you.

REFERENCE

Kipnis D., S.M. Schmidt, C. Swaffin Smith, and I. Wilkinson (1984), 'Patterns of Managerial Influence: Shotgun Managers, Tacticians, and Bystanders', *Organizational Dynamics*, 0112(3), pp. 58–67.

1

It Pays to be
a Persuasive Manager

INTRODUCTION

If you are a manager, you have to get your bosses, subordinates, peers, suppliers, customers, and even the public to do things for you. If you fail, you cannot climb the corporate ladder. If several managers in charge of major business units fail, the entire organization will suffer. Being a manager gives you at least three kinds of power over your subordinates: coercive power, reward power, and legitimate power. If you are an expert in your field, you will wield expert power over your peers and bosses too. If your achievements are such that people look up to you, you will also enjoy referent power over them.

There are two levels at which you need to get others' compliance. The first is getting them to do what they are supposed to do. If they don't play their roles well, you will not be able to perform yours either. The second level, which is much harder, is getting them to change their ideas, attitudes, and behaviour to help your organization cope with competition and the changing environment. When you find that they are unwilling to change even after you explain the need for it and support your argument with solid evidence, you may be tempted to use the coercive and reward power at your disposal. You may get some short-term success, but you must expect sabotage in subtle ways, where and when you least expect it.

There is a smarter way: persuasion. It is an attempt, using one or more means such as reasoning and emotional appeal, to change other people's thinking, attitudes, and eventually behaviour in a way that builds on their cooperation. It is tough and time-consuming but once they are persuaded, you can breathe easy. You don't need to worry about sabotage.

INFURIATING HURDLES

Rahul Saxena is General Manager, Marketing, of a chain of corporate hospitals, all based in metropolitan cities. The hospitals are doing well. A third of the revenue comes from medical tourism and the rest from services rendered to patients within each city. Saxena strongly believes that the way forward is promoting medical tourism targeted at patients from rich countries. To attract those patients, he believes that the company's new hospitals should be set up in small, prosperous, scenically attractive towns, about 30 to 40 km away from big cities. The CEO, however, is quite convinced that a corporate hospital cannot make money unless it is in a large city. She is not willing to test Saxena's idea even in a single small town.

Geeta Pillai has returned to her home town after doing an MBA at a well-known American business school and working abroad for six years. She has taken over her family's processed-foods business. She wants to reduce dependence on skilled and semi-skilled workers, introduce computer-controlled machinery to achieve greater consistency and hygiene levels, and export the products to the US and Europe. Managers and workers, some of whom have been working there for almost twenty years, however, are quite happy with the way things are. There is steady domestic demand for the company's products. The company has always been profitable, and there is no reason to believe that this will change in coming years. They believe that just because she has a foreign MBA, she shouldn't attempt to fix something that is not broken. Geeta feels suffocated. She wants to change the culture of her family's company and make it modern and international. Although she owns the company, she is unable to take it in the direction she wants.

Alok Rathi is the CEO of Golden Harvest Limited, a supermarket chain with about 130 outlets in India. He finds that the margins offered by the multinational makers of high-end breakfast cereals are too low to be profitable. His appeals to them to raise the margins have been unsuccessful. He can, of course, stop stocking those products in his outlets. But he knows that he will lose many high-spending customers to other chains if he does. However, he believes that if all supermarket chains boycotted the products simultaneously, the multinational would have no option but to raise the margins in a matter of three to four weeks. If all chains boycotted the same products, there would be no danger of their losing customers to one another. The CEOs of most other chains, however, are unwilling to go along. They are afraid that they will lose out because unlike Golden Harvest, several of them don't have their own breakfast cereals to promote. Rathi knows that a boycott will work only if everyone participates in it. He is frustrated by the attitude of these CEOs.

There is nothing unusual about any of these individuals or their frustrations with people who are unwilling to cooperate. Every manager with ideas for change faces similar situations. If you are a manager, you *have* to get others to do things. The 'others' could be your bosses, peers, subordinates, suppliers, and customers.

They could be the public—fellow citizens over whom you have no control, no authority. If you cannot get others to do what you want, you cannot go up the corporate ladder. The higher you go, the greater the number and range of people you have to manage and align with your vision. What you do at the highest levels consists almost exclusively of managing people.

SILOS AT MICROSOFT

During the late 1990s, a group of clever graphics experts at Microsoft led by Dick Brass invented ClearType, a way to make text very readable on screen. It was patented; the public praised it. It was developed for e-books, but Microsoft could have used it for every device with a screen. But it took a decade for a fully operational version to get into Windows. Reason? According to Brass, the Windows group put it down falsely claiming that it upset the colour display. The head of Office Products also put it down saying that it was fuzzy and that it gave him headaches. The Vice President for Pocket Devices agreed to support ClearType and use it only if Brass transferred the programme and the programmers to his control.

Similarly, when Brass's group was building the Tablet PC in 2001, the Vice President, Office Products, didn't like the concept because the Tablet needed a stylus and he preferred keyboards. He would not modify the Office application software to work properly with the Tablet. So, although the Tablet, which cost hundreds of millions of dollars to develop, had the support of the top management and its time had come, it was in effect sabotaged.

Dick Brass, who was a Vice President at Microsoft from 1997 to 2004, says he could not persuade the heads of other divisions to support his excellent products. He believes that such silos may destroy the company.

Source: Based on 'Microsoft's Creative Destruction' by Dick Brass in *New York Times,* February 4, 2010, available at http://www.nytimes.com/2010/02/04/opinion/04brass.html?em.

When you have difficulty convincing others to do what you want, you may envy dictators. If you could just order others to do what you thought was good and right, and sit back! Wouldn't that save time and effort wasted in endless discussions and negotiations? You may point to the miraculous growth China's autocratic regime has achieved compared to the inconsistent development India's democratic governments have managed so far. You may admire Jack Welch ('Neutron Jack'), who restructured General Electric, shed about 100,000 jobs in his first four years at the helm, and raised the company's market capitalization from US$13 billion to US$400 billion in twenty years. In fact, you may even try to play the dictator and impose your will on others whenever you find resistance weak. You may succeed for a while, but you should be prepared for nasty surprises.

Managing people is not simple at any level. Often you don't have power over people whose ideas and behaviour you want to control. Even if technically you have power, it is so limited that exercising it and using force to achieve your ends can be ineffective or even counter-productive. Behind a veneer of quiet acceptance there may be strong resistance which leads to sabotage at a critical point later on. The saying that you can lead a horse to water but cannot make it drink captures the limitations of force as a means of getting others to do what you want.

MANAGERS AND POWER

Managers have considerable power over their subordinates and somewhat limited power over their peers and bosses. Such power can vary significantly between managers at the same level in an organization. A manager may wield different kinds of power or different degrees of the same power with different people. Social psychologists John French Jr and Bertram Raven (1959) identify five kinds of such social power:

▶ Coercive power
▶ Reward power
▶ Legitimate power
▶ Expert power
▶ Referent power

The first three are positional power, that is, they derive largely from the position the manager occupies in the organization. Loss of that position can lead to loss of these forms of power. Expert power and referent power generally flow from the wielder's individual accomplishments and hence are independent of the position they hold.

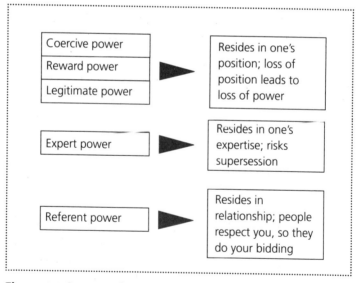

Figure 1.1: Sources of power (based on French and Raven (1959), 'The Bases of Social Power')

Coercive Power

Coercive power is the power to force others to do what you want them to. It stems essentially from your ability to harm another person or group of persons if they don't comply with your wishes. If you wield it, you use the resources of your position to threaten others with unpleasant consequences, such as denial of essential resources. You can, for example, threaten to block a subordinate's promotion or slash his budget if he does not comply with your request for some favour. The efficacy of coercive power depends largely on your ability to prevent others from coming to the rescue of the targets of such power. Many managers are tempted to use coercive power because it is quick and effective in the short term. It fails in the long term because the subordinates do not accept it wholeheartedly; their compliance is forced. They will be looking for an opportunity to get out of it.

Reward Power

Reward power is, in a sense, the opposite of coercive power. Here you get the compliance of subordinates or colleagues by offering them rewards. Rewards, by definition, are things people welcome and enjoy receiving. In an organizational setting, this could be offering your subordinates charge of a highly desirable project, a promotion, a raise, a holiday, and so on to induce them to accept a request. Exercise of reward power by bosses is certainly more acceptable to the subordinates than the exercise of coercive power.

Reward power is not without problems, though. Some independent-minded subordinates may balk at receiving favours with strings attached. Different subordinates may compare the rewards that they have received or have been promised. If the reward that one gets is less significant than that of one's peers, one may not value it at all. Similarly, you may find it difficult or even impossible to make good on some of the promises you made to get a subordinate's compliance because in an organization other forces may prevent it. All this can erode your reward power.

Legitimate Power

Legitimate power is the power that stems from legal or social authority. Whoever holds a superior position in a corporate or social organization has legitimate power over those who are in subordinate positions. Whoever takes up or is elected to a superior position has a right to the power associated with it. Everyone recognizes it. The CEO of a company has certain powers over all its employees. The head of a branch office has certain powers over all the employees at that branch. Most of your coercive power and reward power derives from the resources that your position in the organization gives you.

Any resistance to the demands you make as the holder of legitimate power tends to be feeble because people generally accept the need for rules and regulations to govern social behaviour. There may, however, be strong resistance if certain directions you issue are perceived as blatantly unfair to an individual or group of individuals, or if you try to exert your influence beyond the range of your legitimate power. If, for example, you dismiss an employee for violating a minor company rule, fellow employees may get together and force you to take him back or challenge you in a court of law. Or your boss may override your decision.

Expert Power

Expert power is what individuals derive from their specialist knowledge and skills, irrespective of their position in an organization. The rarer the expertise or the harder it is to acquire, the greater the power it bestows on an individual who possesses it. If you are a subordinate with expertise, you can have tremendous power over your seniors. If you are a boss and you combine legitimate power with expert power, you can command compliance relatively easily. Even among peers you may enjoy power if you have built up a reputation for expertise in a particular field. If, for example, you have a track record of turning around sick companies and have joined the senior management of a sinking company, your colleagues and bosses are likely to heed your advice even when it goes against the majority view.

The main risk in relying on expert power is that expertise can become obsolete and irrelevant when the environment changes. Another risk is that a bigger or better expert may supersede you. In any case, expert power is restricted to the specific area in which a person claims expertise. A highly regarded neurosurgeon may have no more influence in matters related to law or politics than a world-class athlete will have on astrophysics.

Referent Power

Referent power is different from all these. When others admire you, want to be identified with you, and treat your behaviour and beliefs as their point of reference, you have tremendous power over them. They change their behaviour and beliefs to be like you. Your approval is very important to them. Such power often comes from extraordinary achievements in fields such as sports, politics, religion, and entertainment. N.R. Narayana Murthy and Ratan Tata are among India's corporate leaders who wield referent power over millions of people. A.P.J. Kalam, Amitabh Bachchan, Sachin Tendulkar, and Swami Baba Ramdev also enjoy referent power over large numbers of Indians. You don't need to be nationally or internationally prominent to develop referent power; you can have it in your own small circle of influence.

Referent power can be so overwhelming that followers may explain away any counterevidence to their leaders' claim to such exalted status. Advertisers often get celebrities with a huge following to endorse products, services, and ideas because many followers accept their recommendations unquestioningly. By its very nature, referent power is the most effective in a leader manager's repertoire. Carefully cultivated, this personal power can also be the one that lasts the longest.

OBTAINING COMPLIANCE

You generally look for compliance at two levels from those you work with. The first is getting others to do their assigned work so that you can get on with your own work and meet your targets. The others could be your boss, peers, or subordinates. Work in an organization is so interconnected and interdependent that if they don't play their roles well, you will not be able to perform yours either. There are myriad ways in which others can let you down. A boss may, for example, not approve your budget or refuse to assign essential resources when needed; a colleague may fail to deliver her part of a project within the deadline; subordinates may deliver something of unacceptable quality.

You have to make others keep their part of the bargain. This is a constant struggle. Successful players are those who manage to get compliance in all directions at the right time. If you give lack of cooperation from others as the excuse for not meeting your targets, you may satisfy yourself but not the rest of the organization. With a reputation for carpet-blaming, you are unlikely to go very far. The manager who climbs the corporate ladder fast is the one who doesn't complain about non cooperation but ensures support from all sides.

The second level is to get people to change their behaviour which may have worked well and been acceptable so far. In a fast-changing environment, even successful and well-established organizations have to constantly reinvent themselves in order to stay relevant and to overcome the competition. Managers at different levels have to first identify the required change and drive it. This is generally much harder than the first level of compliance unless imminent dangers become visible to everyone. One celebrated instance of a major crisis driving a monumental change is, as Gurcharan Das explains in *India Unbound* (2002), the economic revolution 'a minority government led by a lackluster, seventy-year-old intellectual who was about to retire from active politics' unleashed in India in 1991. Without the humiliating balance of payment crisis of June 1991, argues Das, the Government of India could not have turned its forty-year old socialist legacy on its head so quickly and so effortlessly.

When convinced that a particular measure is needed, many managers use their legitimate power to get it done, at least in those domains which are under their control. They issue circulars or memos explaining the changes they want, the main reasons for the change, and the advantages that result from implementing the change. They believe that this is very reasonable and expect the others to appreciate the move and accept the change. After all, everyone benefits when the company does well. But they are often sorely disappointed. Subordinates who are dictated to may pretend to comply but do everything possible to sabotage the change as in the case of The Dashman Company (see box below).

In order to ensure that the directives are complied with, the management, which may have invested considerable time and resources in formulating them, may try penalties for those who don't fall in line. They will, however, soon realize that threats work only when the targets are very weak or isolated. Weak targets may join forces to form a formidable opposition. As they say, if you borrow US$5,000 from a bank and are unable to return it, you are in trouble; if you borrow US$50 million from a bank and are unable to return it, the bank is in trouble. Numbers strengthen resistance with little risk to individuals.

THE DASHMAN COMPANY

Dashman was an American company that manufactured various types of equipment for the US armed forces. It was highly decentralized with twenty plants in different parts of the country, each functioning largely as an independent unit. In late 1940, Dashman's President judged that procuring essential raw materials might become very difficult. So he created a new post, that of the Vice President of Purchase, and hired an experienced manager from outside the company to coordinate the company's purchases. The President announced his appointment through the usual channels; he also gave the new VP an assistant who had been with the company for many years.

The VP decided to centralize the company's purchase procedures because he felt that without it no meaningful coordination could be done. He wanted the purchase executives in the plants to send him every contract above US$10,000 a week before they signed it. He shared this proposal with the President, who presented it to the board and obtained its approval.

The company's peak buying season was just three weeks away. So as soon as he got the board's approval, the VP wrote to all the purchase executives and asked them to send him all the contracts above US$10,000 a week before signing. In the letter he clearly stated that introducing the new procedure was the board's decision and that it was essential for the company to deal with the anticipated shortage of raw materials. As it was a major departure from the practice in the company, the assistant suggested to the VP that instead of writing to the purchase executives, he should consider visiting the plants and meeting the purchase executives, and discussing the new proposal with them. The VP dismissed it instantly as impractical because he was too busy to travel to different plants.

The purchase executives in most of the plants responded promptly saying essentially that the VP's suggestion was excellent and he could expect their full cooperation. The VP, however, did not receive a single contract from any purchase executive although the company was in the peak buying season. Managers from the headquarters, who visited the plants, reported that all plants were functioning normally.

Source: Summarized from 'The Dashman Company,' case written by Richard S. Meriam, Franklin E. Folts, and George F. Lombard, 1947, *The President and Fellows of Harvard College*, US.

Rewards and incentives have a better chance of obtaining compliance. But even they are unlikely to succeed unless they are perceived as superior to the benefits that people may have to forgo when they adopt the change. Some people are so comfortable with the status quo and dependent on vested interests that the rewards announced by the management may not excite them.

You realize the futility of threats and rewards in getting people to change. You want to bring about change by getting people to understand why those changes are necessary. You initiate discussions, corroborate your proposal with substantial data, and present excellent analyses. You may, however, be surprised that people still don't buy it. They may question the authenticity and integrity of the data. They may condemn your motives. You may become frustrated by either the opposition to your proposals or by the way change plans are sabotaged. Even people who have no better alternatives to propose may criticize the changes being introduced. It may appear that they derive pleasure from pointing out the flaws in the proposed policy initiatives and ignoring the strengths. It can be infuriating when they expect perfection in a policy that replaces the existing policy that everyone detests.

It is obvious that we have to understand the nature of resistance better and develop smarter ways of dealing with it if we want our organizations to triumph in the face of tough competition.

PERSUASION: A WORKING DEFINITION

When we attend a party at a friend's home, it is quite possible to steal small objects without anyone noticing it. Even if the hosts find something missing after the guests leave, it may not be possible to identify who took it away. Questioning any of the guests even indirectly could be embarrassing for the hosts. They would risk offending the guests, who may, as a result, decline any future invitations. In spite of such detection-proof opportunities, most of us avoid stealing. The simple reason is that something within us tells us that it is not right to betray the trust that the friend placed in our integrity. If we stole something, we would be troubled by a sense of guilt, irrespective of whether there was any chance of being found out. The decision not to steal from a friend's house is driven internally because we have firmly bought into the idea that it is wrong.

When our actions are driven by such strong convictions, not

necessarily moral as in the example above, there is no need for external monitoring. This is the ideal for change management in organizations. People should do things not because they are afraid of the unpleasant consequences of nonconformity or because of the rewards of conformity, but because they are convinced that they are doing the right things. The process of taking people to that level of conviction, however, is neither easy nor quick. In fact, it can be exasperatingly slow. Nonetheless, it is the only long-term strategy that has a good chance of sustained success. And this is the persuasive manager's goal. Rewards and punishments are of course there in the background; but you must achieve others' compliance through persuasion.

What is persuasion? Persuasion is such a common and central human activity that it is as difficult to define it as 'democracy' and 'religion'. Different scholars have defined it differently, highlighting the various facets of this human activity. For our purposes, let's treat it as an attempt, using means such as reasoning and emotional appeal, to change others' thinking, attitudes, and eventually behaviour in a way that builds on their willing cooperation.

PERSUASION DEFINED

1. To persuade is 'to move by argument, entreaty, or expostulation to a belief, position, or course of action.' (Merriam Webster Online)
2. Persuasion is 'the presenting of inducements or winning arguments to a person to induce him to do or believe something.' (Oxford)
3. Persuasion is 'the process by which a person's attitudes or behaviour are, without duress, influenced by communications from other people.' (*Encyclopaedia Britannica*)
4. Persuasion is 'language or non-verbal behaviour intended to change people's beliefs, opinions, attitudes, and/or behaviour.' (*Encyclopaedia of Human Behaviour*)

That persuasion is an attempt, a deliberate activity, distinguishes it from many forms of influence. You may influence someone without your knowing it or without any attempt on your part. Imagine, for example, that you are a policeman on your way to work. You are in your uniform, standing at a bus stop waiting for a bus. You are not trying to persuade anyone to do anything. But your *presence* there may influence the way bus drivers and passengers behave. Drivers may, for example, stop exactly at the bus stop, rather than beyond or ahead of it, as they often do. Passengers may come out of the bus in a more orderly fashion than usual. Similarly, the absence of a teacher can influence the way children behave in a classroom. Influence, therefore, can be a major factor in your persuasion efforts. We will look at it more closely in the next chapter, when we deal with ethos.

That persuasion attempts to change behaviour by bringing about a change in ideas and attitudes distinguishes it from coercion or pressure. Central to persuasion is the change in ideas and attitudes. When these change, behaviour follows suit. When coerced or pressured, people may change their external behaviour to escape pain. It doesn't imply a change of mind or attitude. The moment pressure is removed, the person may revert to her previous behaviour, rather like the way an inflated balloon held underwater with your palm rises to the surface the moment you tilt your palm. The advantage of persuasion is that the change of behaviour is sustained by changed ideas and attitudes and when there is no dissonance between the two.

Related to the change in ideas and attitudes is the willing cooperation of the person being persuaded. In genuine persuasion, the persuadee retains his choice. He is not tricked into changing his ideas or attitudes. The persuader meets his concerns and objections, if any, before the change takes place. The persuader and persuadee work together to arrive at the new ideas, attitudes, and behaviours. In such collaborative efforts, the persuader herself might experience change. It is this aspect of genuine persuasion which distinguishes it from deceitful manipulation (Chapter 9). This does not, however, mean that the persuader will invariably give the potential persuadee a full account of the consequences of the change in behaviour that the persuader is seeking. Again, we shall take a more detailed look at the process of persuasion and the role of strategy in subsequent chapters.

ADVANTAGES OF PERSUASION

Changing minds and attitudes is tough. People often have certain ideas so firmly fixed in their minds that they may consider it unnecessary to think of alternatives, let alone accept any. Similarly, their bias in favour of or against certain things can stand in the way of even an open-ended review of some of their ideas. At times, the mere mention of a word or phrase such as 'capitalism' or 'pre-marital sex' can trigger the sudden closure of a person's mind. That is why a persuader needs time, patience, and a strategic approach to accomplish good quality persuasion.

PRESSURE VERSUS PERSUASION

Thaw with her gentle persuasion is more powerful than Thor with his hammer. The one melts, the other breaks into pieces.

—*Henry David Thoreau*

Not brute force but only persuasion and faith are the kings of this world.

—*Thomas Carlyle*

Why should you invest your time and effort in persuasion when there are shortcuts and examples of successful coercion—dictators who have ruled countries as well as companies with an iron hand? As we have briefly noted above, many managers are tempted to use their legitimate power along with the coercive and reward power that goes with it to get their subordinates and, in some cases, peers to do what they want. The advantage of opting instead for persuasion is twofold. First, the change is likely to hold without active and constant monitoring by the persuader. Second, the quality of compliance will be higher because it will be wholehearted. It is not surprising then that Dwight D. Eisenhower, US General and 34th president, stated: 'I would rather try to persuade a man to go along, because once I have persuaded him, he will stick. If I scare him, he will stay just as long as he is scared, and then he is gone.'

It is true that if you are powerless, your persuasive power is also likely to be weak. As we shall see in the next chapter, the persuader's power is a major factor in the success of his persuasive efforts. Trouble starts when people rely on power alone to get compliance.

On October 14, 2008, for example, Jet Airways laid off 800 flight attendants. The following day the CEO and Executive Director announced at a press conference that they would terminate the services of another 1,100 employees including 200 engineers and managers. They declared: 'It is an unfortunate decision, which all of us in the company regret but it is an attempt to save the company and the jobs of the remaining employees.' The company had a very good reason to lay off the employees. It also had the legitimate power. Before announcing the lay off, however, the top management didn't think it necessary to talk to the employees to find a way out of the unsustainably heavy losses the company was making. The stunned employees ran to powerful political leaders and pulled all sorts of strings. On October 16, the chairman, Naresh Goyal, publicly announced that the company was taking back all the laid-off employees. In spite of all the melodrama accompanying his public announcement, the company lost face and goodwill.

It appears that the temptation to rely on power rather than persuasion is too strong to resist in spite of numerous examples of its futility.

CONCLUSION

In this chapter we have argued that managers who fail to get compliance from people at different levels weaken their own and their company's prospects. We have also noted that there are two levels at which managers need to get others to comply. The first is getting them to honour existing commitments. The second is making them change their behaviour to help the organization cope with competition and the changing business environment. Faced with the need to get people to change, many managers use their coercive, reward, and legitimate power rather than persuasion. Relying on persuasion is a better idea because it changes others' thinking, attitudes, and eventually behaviour in a way that builds on their willing cooperation. The process is tough and time-consuming, but it protects managers and organizations from nasty surprises.

LESSONS LEARNT

▶ Getting others' compliance is crucial for managerial success and professional growth.
▶ The first level of compliance is getting others to perform their roles.

- ▶ The second level of compliance is getting others to change their behaviour.
- ▶ Managers are often tempted to use positional power to bring about changes.
- ▶ Persuasion is tough and time-consuming, but a superior alternative.

In the next chapter we shall take a close look at the process and principles of persuasion. We shall identify the major persuasion factors, the conditions under which persuasion takes place, and a few common persuasion techniques. In the rest of the book, we shall explore ways of using these techniques in our quest for compliance from our subordinates, peers, bosses, and suppliers.

REFERENCE

Das, Gurcharan. (2002) *India Unbound: From Independence to the Global Information Age*. New Delhi: Penguin.

'French, J. R. P. Jr, and B. Raven (1959). The Bases of Social Power.' In D. Cartwright (ed.) *Studies in Social Power*. Ann Arbor, MI: University of Michigan Press, pp. 150–67.

2

The Basics of Persuasion

INTRODUCTION

Is persuasion an art? Or is it a science? It is difficult to answer this question one way or the other. Perhaps persuasion is a bit of both. Our objective in this chapter is to identify the *basics of persuasion* so that we can use them systematically in situations presented in the following chapters.

Reasoning appears in all forms of persuasion. Logical reasoning works best when the persuader has credibility and the persuadee's emotional state is aligned with it. Both these factors reduce resistance to rational persuasion, often by dulling the mind.

The heart of persuasion is framing because whether a persuasion attempt will succeed or not depends largely on whether the compliance request is presented in a way that matches the potential persuadee's needs and beliefs. This boils down to their perceiving the proposal as benefiting them in some way. The benefit could be fulfilment of a need or vindication of a belief that gives them satisfaction.

In this chapter we shall also identify the most common moves we make to persuade others.

THE PERSUASION FACTORS

More than two thousand years ago Aristotle captured the fundamentals of persuasion in three words:

- ▶ Ethos
- ▶ Pathos
- ▶ Logos

Although Aristotle was referring, in his *Rhetoric*, specifically to the means of persuasion in public speaking, these three factors can be said to underlie all kinds of persuasion. The techniques, tactics, and strategies of persuasion that other scholars have identified down the centuries derive from one or more of these factors.

Ethos

Ethos is the most important and most powerful of the three persuasion factors. In fact, Aristotle considers it almost the overriding factor in persuasion. Ethos is, as we shall see later, what makes one a persuasive manager rather than a run-of-the-mill manager who uses some persuasion techniques effectively.

Ethos is nothing but the product of a persuader's character. If the persuader is perceived as credible and fair-minded, it is easy for her to persuade others, especially in contexts where indisputable knowledge is not possible and there is room for doubt. We tend to trust people whose character we believe to be good and moral. Once we trust someone, we may accept an idea she proposes, even if we don't fully understand it because we expect her not to exploit our ignorance. Her credibility is enhanced if she has developed and demonstrated expertise in the field in which she is trying to persuade us. But expertise alone may not make a person's advice persuasive; we may have a persistent, subconscious fear that she may use her expertise for her own benefit at our expense. We may hold out and refuse to be persuaded by an expert we don't consider trustworthy. Nothing can beat a combination of trustworthiness and expertise. Any opposition we may have to a suggestion will probably melt like wax when the persuasion effort comes from a trustworthy expert.

DOUG SANDERS HITS A WINNER

Mark McCormack's company, International Management Group (IMG), represented the American golfer Doug Sanders and organized all his matches. Once, however, Sanders played an exhibition match in Canada without involving either McCormack or anyone else in his company. None of them knew anything about that match because Sanders had made all the arrangements himself. And, apparently, he was paid in cash. There was, therefore, no realistic chance of IMG claiming and getting any commission from the match. A week after the event, however, McCormack received an envelope from Sanders. There was no letter inside, only cash—IMG's commission for the match in Canada.

As Sanders was flamboyant and far too controversial to give comfort to his agent, many people wondered why McCormack chose to represent him. This story was his reply to them because that single incident revealed Sanders's trustworthiness to McCormack in a way that won him over for life.

Source: Mark McCormack, *What they don't Teach you at Harvard Business School: Notes from a Street-smart Executive*, 1986, New York: Bantam. pp. 3–4.

We can extend ethos to include physical attractiveness. Good looking people tend to be more persuasive than plain looking ones. It is as though attractive people can be trusted to say and do the right thing. Their words and deeds are often accepted without much critical scrutiny. Many targets of persuasion go along mindlessly, like the Pavlovian dog, when the source of the persuasion attempt is physically attractive. This has been confirmed again and again through common experience as well as experiments in environments as varied as primary schools, courtrooms, and shopping malls. How very unfortunate for most of us!

While good looks help, what really matters in getting compliance in major change initiatives is the persuader's character. That is what helped Mahatma Gandhi persuade the tallest leaders of his time such as Pandit Jawaharlal Nehru, Sardar Vallabhbhai Patel, and Maulana Abul Kalam Azad to embrace non-violence in India's independence struggle.

Pathos

When a speaker arouses his listeners' emotions in favour of himself or against his opponent, he is in effect using pathos to persuade them. Aristotle recognizes that our judgement is coloured by emotional states such as grief, joy, friendliness, and hostility. A smart persuader uses this insight to sway the audience in the direction he wants. Aristotle lists the kind of people who arouse friendliness in us: people who admire us; people who are pleasant, good-tempered, and not critical of our faults; people who have a sense of humour; people who are neat and well dressed; and people who are like us (for example, those who belong to the same region, religion, club, political party, and so on) and have similar interests provided they are not competing with us for the same resources. Several modern scholars (see a summary by J.K. Burgoon and others, 2002) have confirmed the power of similarity in persuasion attempts.

If you get to know that the person who is trying to sell you a product or service is from your hometown or from your old school, you may not blindly buy it but are likely to be influenced favourably towards him. You may go out of your way to accommodate his requests in a way you may not for someone who offers a superior product or service. This is the power of similarity in persuasion.

We can divide emotions into two broad categories: negative and positive. Fear, anger, disgust, guilt, and envy are a few of the negative emotions. Pride, joy, hope, and compassion are among the positive ones. Arousing any one or more of these emotions in support of our proposal can persuade our audience to accept or reject a particular course of action. We may, for example, work up our audience's fear of certain consequences to dissuade them from doing something we don't want them to. Or, we may excite their pride in something to get them to attempt a specific course of action, which they might otherwise avoid. Well-delivered appeals to emotions work because they soften the audience's resistance or reduce their ability to process critical and relevant information.

EMOTION IN PERSUASION

In 1964, when President Lyndon B. Johnson wanted to persuade businessmen to give greater opportunities to Afro-Americans, he tried emotion rather than reason. He quoted the example of Zephyr Wright, his family's housekeeper. He said that she was a college graduate who had worked for them for about twenty years. Yet when she came to Washington from Texas, she didn't know where she could buy a cup of coffee or find a bathroom. She had to take three or four hours out of her travel time to locate a place where she could sit down and buy a meal. All because of her skin colour. Would you want that to happen to your wife, mother, or sister, asked Johnson.
Source: P. F. Boller, *Presidential Anecdotes*, 1996, New York: Oxford University Press, p. 322.

Why do employees in many firms work beyond office hours for no extra pay? Often the simple reason is that their leader has been able to arouse their pride in their organization to such a degree that they are willing to do anything to defeat their rivals. They may be number one now, and they want to fend off challenges to their position from rivals who are close on their heels. Or they may be number two or three, and they have set their heart on becoming number one. Such devotion to work is due to emotional persuasion, never rational persuasion.

A LUXURY RIDE INTO TURBULENCE

It was widely reported that on November 19, 2008, the CEOs of Chrysler, Ford, and General Motors (Robert L. Nardelli, Alan R. Mulally, and Rick Wagoner) flew into Washington to attend the hearing of the House Committee on Financial Services. They were hoping to persuade the lawmakers to approve an additional US$25 billion to bail out the American automobile industry, which was on the verge of bankruptcy.

Instead of asking them for evidence to justify why taxpayers' money should be given to them, Brad Sherman, a leading member of the committee, grilled them on how they arrived in Washington. All three had come from Detroit, each flying his company's luxury corporate jet.

There was nothing new in CEOs of large companies, with operations in dozens of countries, flying private jets to save time. But in this context, as they begged for a bailout, their action evoked negative emotions in the lawmakers, colouring their judgement while considering the CEOs' data and rational arguments.

Source: Based on reports in *The New York Times*.

Emotion is often looked down upon in the corporate world as an unworthy candidate for consideration. It is as though emotions belong to one's private or personal world. But this is far from reality. Emotions have an important role to play whenever people have to be persuaded to accept a product, service, or an idea.

Logos

When persuasion results from logical reasoning, we can say that the persuader is using logos. The persuader may use either inductive or deductive logic, both of which have certain strengths and weaknesses.

Inductive reasoning is also called paradigmatic thinking or examples-based reasoning. In this kind of reasoning, we look at several similar instances, identify a pattern, and assert that something similar can be expected in a fresh instance. Here is an example. We find that Rohit smoked 20 to 25 cigarettes a day for five years. Bhaskaran did the same thing. So did Nirmesh. All three developed lung cancer. Swaroop has been smoking 20 to 25 cigarettes a day for two years. If we conclude that he is likely to develop lung cancer in the next three years, we use inductive reasoning. The larger the number of examples and the greater the consistency of the pattern of results, the stronger is the persuasive power of the inductive conclusion. But at times, we jump to a conclusion based on a single experience. For instance, I get cheated by a Malayali vendor at a railway station in Mumbai. I should not jump to the conclusion that all Malayali vendors are cheats, but unfortunately we often reach such untenable conclusions.

Deductive reasoning is also called rhetorical syllogism. Here is an example:

▶ Major premise: All men are mortal.
▶ Minor premise: Socrates is a man.

▶ Conclusion/deduction: Therefore Socrates is mortal.

If you accept the general premise that all men are mortal and the particular premise that Socrates is a man, you have no choice but to accept the conclusion that Socrates is mortal. If the general statement is universally acceptable, as in this case, there is no need to restate it before coming to the conclusion that Socrates is mortal because he is a man. All we need to say is that Socrates is mortal. We can take for granted the syllogism that leads to this conclusion.

If a premise is factually wrong or merely a matter of personal opinion, the deduction will not persuade those who dispute it. Assume that you are the chairman of a company. There are three strong contenders, including a woman, for the CEO's position that has recently become vacant. If you start from the premise that women do not make good CEOs and conclude that therefore the woman candidate should not be made your company's CEO, your major premise is your personal opinion. You are unlikely to persuade the members of the Board of Directors to ignore the woman candidate if they don't subscribe to your major premise. If, however, they also believe in it, they will readily go along with your conclusion.

This brings us to the limitations of persuasion through logical reasoning: on its own it is unlikely to make us very persuasive although it appears to be very powerful and managers frequently employ it. Deductive arguments fall flat when the audience rejects either the major premise, or the minor premise, or both. Similarly, inductive arguments fail to persuade those audience members who question the number and quality of examples from which we arrive at that conclusion. They could say that the number of samples is too small to arrive at anything conclusive, or that the ones collected are skewed. Thus logical reasoning is like a perfectly healthy seed—it will sprout and grow into a plant only if it finds itself in moist soil.

In spite of the limitations of logical reasoning, we constantly encounter it because we are rational beings looking for logic in everything we do. The content of persuasion comes from reasoning, but it works only when the mind has been prepared favourably by ethos and pathos.

> If you would persuade, you must appeal to interest rather than intellect.
>
> —*Benjamin Franklin*

MAJOR PERSUASIVE MOVES

We now need to examine the major moves we make to influence others favourably and to persuade them. We call them moves because they are not sure-fire recipes but broad directions we take to be persuasive. As we go on, we will also use the terms 'techniques' and 'tactics' to refer to some aspects of these persuasive moves. Here, we can draw upon a number of scholars who have systematically identified these moves over the years. In the following discussion, however, we shall depend mainly on the work of David Kipnis, Gary Yukl, and Robert Cialdini.

Here are the most commonly employed persuasive moves:

▶ Making oneself likeable
▶ Leveraging authority
▶ Creating indebtedness
▶ Stroking the target's ego
▶ Playing on herd instinct

- ▶ Getting small commitments
- ▶ Appealing to shared values
- ▶ Engaging the target in consultation
- ▶ Using inductive and deductive reasoning

Our descriptions here will be brief. We shall elaborate on them when we focus, in the later chapters, on how to persuade people at different levels.

Ethos	Pathos	Logos
▶ Making oneself likeable ▶ Leveraging authority	▶ Creating indebtedness ▶ Stroking the ego ▶ Playing on herd instinct ▶ Getting small commitments ▶ Appealing to shared values	▶ Engaging target in consultation ▶ Using inductive and deductive reasoning

Figure 2.1: Major Persuasive Moves with Links to Persuasion Factors

Making Oneself Likeable

It is difficult to say no to a friend or a person you like. You like him so much that you don't want to risk losing his company or your special relationship with him. You are worried that you will lose him if you decline even an unreasonable request from him. But there is something mutual about this. You believe that when you please him you have a hold on him.

Making ourselves likeable should, therefore, strengthen our personal appeal and help us become more persuasive. The first step towards it is analysing what makes us likeable and to whom. If we figure that out, we may be able to tone down, if not eliminate, some features of our personality that put people off and enhance those features that draw people to us. What is certain is that every one of us has some features that others like in us and make us appealing to them.

As we have noted above, good looks can make people likeable and give them a tremendous advantage. We instinctively try not to disappoint such people, especially if they belong to the opposite sex, even when they are strangers and we may never meet them again. Sadly, most of us will be right in blaming our stars for not putting us on this easy path to persuasiveness. But all is not lost. We can reduce the disadvantage of plain looks to some extent by paying attention to our self-presentation. Careful grooming that leads to a confident bearing can go a long way. Equally useful is polished and polite behaviour that is marked by concern for others' welfare.

Another factor that makes people likeable and trustworthy is similarities. We tend to like people who are like us: people from the same linguistic or religious community, from the same village or town, from the same school or college, having the same passions or hobbies, and so on. It is therefore a good idea to find out if we share with our targets any characteristics that will make them like us, or at least, treat us with special consideration.

While good looks and similarities are useful, we would be foolish to rely on them for success in persuasion. We may not have those attributes or they may not work on the people we want to persuade. So we have to look for something that is more feasible, and within everyone's reach: warm and friendly behaviour. This generally makes us likeable. We're not talking here about wearing pretty masks as part of a persuasive strategy. We are talking about the need to look beyond our noses and take genuine interest in the people we interact with. If we are warm and friendly, we have a good chance of persuading even strangers to do what we want. Confidence tricksters know this very well and exploit it to make perfect strangers willingly part with money. We can use it to do good instead.

Leveraging Authority

Every day we are buffeted by news of a wide spectrum of crimes. Severe punishments, including long prison sentences and execution, don't seem to deter the perpetrators. Yet, the amazing thing is not that there are crimes but that there are so few crimes. The vast majority of people in all countries abide by the law of the land. Violators are a small minority. It shows that people by and large defer to authority. You may be able to persuade people to do what you want by relying on your authority over them or appealing to a higher authority if your own authority is not adequate.

As mentioned in Chapter 1, legitimate power generally enables you to get compliance through coercion and rewards. If you enjoy expert or referent power, preferably a combination of the two, your persuasive efforts will have an excellent success rate. What power does is to dispose the target favourably towards being persuaded. Complying with authority usually has the advantage of peace of mind, and in many cases, short-term and long-term rewards. Defying authority usually leads to penalties. It's easy to see why authority is such a powerful influence.

The power to change others when they accept a person's authority as an expert or a leader who sets standards is remarkable.

There are also many instances of prominent people with entrenched positions giving it all up when asked to do so by certain religious leaders whom they follow and revere.

Even if you don't have any of these powers, you may still be able to get compliance relatively easily if you are associated with or have access to those who have power. If, for example, you are the personal assistant to the managing director, your position in the hierarchy is very low with no managerial power; but you can easily persuade many senior managers to do anything you suggest because you control access to the top boss. Spouses of leaders and bosses may exert considerable authority without any legitimate, expert, or referent power whatsoever. The close association with powerful people gives them power which others defer to.

When you are unable to persuade someone at your level, you may find it useful to take the matter to a person (such as a common boss, the other person's boss, a corporate leader, or a religious figure) who is highly regarded by your target. That is what Bharat Parekh did (see box below, The Long Shortcut) when he could not get managers at Apex Ltd to build the HT Transformer he had ordered. In such cases, you leverage authority, but not your own.

THE LONG SHORTCUT

In the early nineties, I was looking after purchases for my company's new cement projects. In 1992, we needed a switchyard for an upcoming plant. The heart of the switchyard would be a custom-built Rs 200 million HT transformer. Apex Ltd, which took our order, promised to deliver the switchyard in twelve months. That fitted our plant-commissioning schedule perfectly.

Soon the export market opened up unexpectedly and Apex was flooded with orders for HT Transformers.

Apex's division that had booked our order was to source the HT transformer from another division, a separate profit centre. When I checked, a couple of months after we placed the order, both the divisions assured me that everything was fine and that I shouldn't worry about the delivery. I was not convinced. So I visited the shop-floor of the manufacturing division; I also talked to the planning and manufacturing teams. They had not allocated to our transformer a manufacturing slot in their production plan. Unless they did it immediately there was no way they could deliver the transformer by the deadline. Their sole focus seemed to be on the lucrative export orders. In spite of my best efforts, I could not get a firm commitment from the division president about allocating a slot immediately to our transformer.

I was worried that this would indefinitely delay the commissioning of our new plant. So I decided to change my strategy. Why not meet Apex's MD? If I could somehow meet him, I felt confident that I would be able to convince him that his company ought to honour the promised deadline. If he intervened , they would not dare delay our order. But meeting him was virtually impossible because he was not only the head of a very large company but also a towering figure in the industry, while I was a mere Purchase Manager. I was not sure his office would let me speak to him.

With great difficulty and some guile I persuaded the MD's secretary to put my call through to him. I told him that I wanted to meet him for just a few minutes at a time most convenient for him. He sensed that there was something wrong and wanted me to talk to him right away. I did because I was thorough with all the details. I also mentioned the high regard we held his company in. He understood the gravity of the situation. He assured me that Apex would come back to us within days. On the third day, we received a letter from the President of the Transformer Division confirming allocation of

Creating Indebtedness

In a blogpost entitled 'Doing Favors versus Being of Service,' Paula Langguth Ryan narrates an incident that took place in a church in Florida. At the end of the service, a man named Eddie stood up, moved to the front, and asked the congregation if he could whistle a song for them. No one objected. He whistled and slapped on his thighs. The entire congregation joined in and clapped along. Once the song was over, Eddie told them that his family was struggling and that he would be grateful if any of them liked his song and could help him in any way. There was an initial hesitation but then people opened up and donated generously. Ryan adds that Eddie gave freely, and the congregation responded in the same spirit.

Of course, Eddie gave freely. But he was employing one of the most powerful persuasive moves to get strangers to open their purse-strings. When he whistled for them and got them to join in, he made them feel indebted to him for the entertainment he provided. It is true that he did not set a price, either before or after the song, for his service. But it would be difficult for them to walk away carrying a burden of debt to this man when it was so simple to remove it by dropping a dollar or two into his hat. As the equity theory of John Stacey Adams (1965) states, people often try to remove such imbalances. Donating a few dollars did it for these churchgoers.

Eddie's unsolicited whistling reminds us of a scene that is played out every day on many passenger trains in India. A person starts singing loudly as the train starts moving out of a station. At the end of the song the singer approaches the passengers for money. Many passengers willingly give the singer some money. The simple reason is that they have received a service and it would be churlish not to pay for it. That it is an unsolicited service, that they couldn't help listening to the song, doesn't make any real difference. The singer leverages the passengers' sense of debt to persuade them to part with money as a means of restoring the balance.

Creation of a burden of indebtedness in others through 'free' gifts and favours to bolster one's persuasiveness is widely practised in all walks of life, including the corporate one. It is amazing how much a bottle of wine or a free meal can achieve. Drug companies provide a particularly telling example. While most doctors assert that small gifts don't influence their professional practice, Stephanie Saul shows in her *The New York Times* article (Drug Makers Pay for Lunch as They Pitch, July 28, 2006) that drug companies that provide sandwiches and small gifts to doctors and their staff notice a significant jump in the sales of their prescription drugs. Somehow, people who receive gifts feel an obligation to return something bigger to the gift giver.

We can extend the scope of this move to include bargaining and explicit or implicit exchange: if you do X for me, I shall do Y for you. The principle is the same. We do things to ensure equity and balance.

Stroking The Target's Ego

We can create another kind of powerful indebtedness in targets by stroking their egos with praise and even flattery. We all crave praise, appreciation, and approval. This is partly because we tend to judge our self-worth in a competitive world based on how others perceive us and partly because appreciation is in short supply, almost choked by abundant criticism. When someone offers us praise or appreciation for something we are or have achieved, they boost our egos and this gives us tremendous pleasure. This praise makes us indebted to them psychologically in a deeper way than material gifts. It prompts us to reciprocate by doing what the admirer asks us to do. The influence of praise, well delivered, is so subtle that we may not even realize it.

> I have yet to find the man, however exalted his station, who did not do better work and put forth greater effort under a spirit of approval than under a spirit of criticism.
>
> —*Charles M. Schwab.*

Praise works at all levels. Even those who are idolized by everyone, such as champion athletes and film stars, thirst for adulation. But stroking egos does not automatically secure the target's compliance. You still need to find and present a good reason why the target should do what you ask them to. But when you flatter their egos, you soften them and dilute their potential resistance, making persuasion easier.

Here, it is important to note the difference between praise and flattery. Praise is genuine in the sense that you believe that the target deserves it. The target also accepts it as praise if she believes that she deserves it. Flattery is praise that you know the target does not deserve. If the target also believes so and realizes that you are using it as a ploy to extract a particular response, you run the risk of alienating her. In spite of that risk, blatant flattery often works as efficiently as genuine praise because we are so desperate for appreciation that we are reluctant to stop its soothing music, even when we know we don't deserve it. 'We are,' says Robert Cialdini, 'phenomenal suckers for flattery.' As a matter of persuasive strategy, however, it is best for managers to rely on genuine praise and appreciation.

Genuine praise is usually specific. If you say, after attending a presentation by a colleague, 'your opening of the presentation was striking,' or 'I was thoroughly impressed by the way you handled that tough question from the VP,' she is likely to treat your praise as genuine. If, however, you tell the same colleague, 'your presentation was fantastic,' she may or may not take it as a genuine compliment especially if there were 'dry patches' in the presentation.

But, even genuine praise can put a discerning target on guard if it is used as a technique just ahead of a persuasion attempt. If you want to be a persuasive manager, you need to make it a habit to look out for things you can praise in others. Praise without expecting anything in return. And don't wait until they climb Mount Everest barefoot before you find in them something you can praise. When you regularly stroke the egos of people you work with, you will be building up a psychological credit with them, which you can cash in at the time of actual persuasion efforts.

Playing on Herd Instinct

We like to think that we are different from and superior to the majority of people. We may criticise others' beliefs and actions. But strangely enough, we feel uncomfortable when we have to behave differently from the crowd. Effective persuaders can play on our herd instinct, our need to keep up with the Joneses, to get us to do what they want. Robert Cialdini calls it the rule of social proof or social validation.

It is common for volunteers of NGOs seeking donations to tell us how much other people in our social category have contributed. We tend to treat that as a benchmark and try to exceed or at least match it. When a garments shop assistant tells us that everyone is buying a particular design, we go ahead and choose it because we believe we won't go wrong. Few of us have the guts to wear clothes that are no longer fashionable even if they are comfortable and we look good in them. Few of us will stop at a red traffic light early in the morning or late in the evening when traffic is thin and there is no police supervision, if everyone else ignores it. Similarly, few of us will dare jump the traffic light if all other motorists stop. *Whatever we claim, most of us hate standing out from the crowd.* Smart persuaders make use of this insight.

Some managers who convene meetings talk to some members in advance, discuss certain issues with them, and get their acceptance. When these people talk in support of the convener's position, the others tend to go along unless they have strong objection. Behind such acquiescence is our discomfort at being the odd one out. This behaviour is particularly evident when the number of attendees is high at a meeting. Once the meeting is over, the silent dissenters may, in their informal chats with their friends, describe some of those decisions as silly.

That everyone else is doing something is not a good enough reason why we should be doing it. However, a manager may be able to persuade his bosses, peers, and subordinates to do something by taking precisely this line. Children do so to persuade parents. It works most of the time. Of course, when we claim that others are doing something, it is important that we are truthful. If we are not, we will lose credibility and harm ourselves in the long term.

CROWD APPEAL

The Director General of Police (DGP) of one of the BIMARU states (Bihar, Madhya Pradesh, Rajasthan, and Uttar Pradesh) was very keen on introducing the system of police commissioners in the major cities of the state. Influenced apparently by the Indian Administrative Service officers working with him, the Chief Minister was not open to the idea. So the DGP asked his colleagues to talk favourably about the system of police commissioners whenever they had an opportunity to meet the Chief Minister.

When an Additional DGP had an opportunity, he told the Chief Minister that all states had police commissioners except the BIMARU states. Not introducing the system of police commissioners, he added, would deny their state membership of the group of progressive states.

The Additional DGP told a group of police officers at a conference later that not long after his meeting, the Chief Minister approved the introduction of the system of police commissioners in that state. The officer was convinced that the Chief Minister was influenced at least partly by his reference to BIMARU and progressive states. (Names withheld)

Getting Small Commitments

In his book, *Influence: The Psychology of Persuasion*, Cialdini talks about a trick called 'throwing a lowball' that he has seen some salesmen at car dealerships use to virtually trap potential car buyers. When a prospect shows interest in a particular model, the salesman offers her a very good price, a few hundred dollars below the local competitors' price. She is encouraged to drive the car for a day to get a feel and to show it to her family, friends, and neighbours. Once she decides to buy and starts filling in relevant documents, the salesman's manager or the bank that finances the purchase 'detects' an error in the salesman's calculation. The sale is disallowed because, the customer is told, at that price the dealership will lose money. When the error is corrected, the price is not very different from what other dealers charge. She has every right to walk away now that the price is higher than what she was promised originally, but in most such cases customers pay the extra amount demanded and buy the car, although now there is no advantage in buying from that particular dealer. The simple reason for this behaviour is that the customers have committed themselves to buying the car. They want to honour that commitment. They have gone too far with the purchase procedure to walk away from it with an easy conscience.

While this is a dishonest way of exploiting customers, it illustrates a powerful approach to persuasion (also called foot-in-the-door technique) that can be used for noble objectives. The move consists of getting a small commitment from the target before he is asked to make a major commitment. The first commitment, which is often so small and harmless that he makes it without thinking hard about its consequences. It gives him a self-image that he wants to protect. He would not want to do anything that would hurt it. The power of this commitment is especially strong if it has been made in public or in writing. The first commitment could be as simple as contributing to a discussion on a proposed initiative such as setting up a temporary crèche for the children of construction workers on company premises. Once you state that it is a good idea, you will find it extremely difficult not to contribute financially to the project later on when employees are encouraged to contribute to the venture.

It is also useful to recognize that this need for consistency is the reason behind people's resistance to change their religious, political, and cultural attitudes. They have taken a stand, often publicly, and they feel obliged to stick to it even when evidence makes it unsustainable. They may question the validity of the evidence and dismiss it rather than change their attitudes. Managers who want to bring about changes in their organizations should, therefore, take into account the need people feel to behave consistently with their existing beliefs and commitments.

Appealing to Shared Values

Every community—family, club, village, school, town, country, and so on—has certain shared values irrespective of its size and diversity. Members cherish them so deeply that they are willing to make sacrifices to uphold them. Football coaches and school principals appeal to shared values as frequently and as successfully as corporate bosses and political leaders. The leader, thus, gets the followers to do something remarkable, which they may not otherwise attempt at all.

The shared values often refer to pride in an existing reputation. Employees of a fast-food joint may be proud of its reputation for not keeping any customer waiting for more than five minutes for service even at peak hours. Employees of a bakery may be proud of its reputation for making the best bread in town. All members of such an organization are so proud of that reputation and so committed to maintaining it that the leader may be able to get them to go the extra mile to avoid damaging it. The persuasive power comes not from the leader but from the values that the community upholds. The leader merely appeals to them.

A leader may be able to go a step further and generate a new vision that binds the whole community when there is no existing reputation to cherish or vision to follow. This is harder. But inspirational leaders do exactly that. HCL Technologies CEO Vineet Nayar (2010), for example, put employees ahead of customers in his attempt to deal with the 2007–09 global recession. He successfully sold his vision to his followers, 'nearly tripled [his company's] annual revenues, doubled its market capitalization, [and it was] ranked India's best employer by Hewitt' (p. 94). Once followers buy into a vision, it will be possible for leaders to get them to do extraordinary things, even difficult things, to achieve that vision. This is a two-stage persuasion move. The first stage is getting the followers to accept a powerful new vision. The second is relying on that vision to seek their willing compliance. If the first stage is built well, the second stage is relatively easy.

Engaging the Target in Consultation

Consultation is one of the smartest moves available to persuade people at all levels: bosses, peers, and subordinates. It works with suppliers and customers too. It consists of sharing a problem with your target and seeking her help in resolving it. It creates an environment in which you may be able to share with her how you propose to solve the problem and invite her response and suggestions for the best solution. She may have no suggestion at all, in which case, she may not be able to criticise or hold out against your proposed solution. If she offers one that reflects her resistance to your proposal, you may be able to point out some of the practical problems she may have missed out. What happens in this process is collaborative solving of a problem rather than one person trying to get a reluctant target on board. The persuadee may not even realize that she is being persuaded. Consultation virtually eliminates resistance and introduces collaboration.

There is, of course, a big risk in using consultation for persuasion. You cannot always predict the outcome. You may find yourself moving far away from the position you want to hold. This is because the target may suggest solutions well beyond what you had anticipated. Having opened the door to consultation you cannot suddenly slam it in the target's face because you don't like the solution she proposes. You have to either accept it or show her the flaws in her solution. Consultation, therefore, is not suitable if you are sure you want to bring the target to a particular, non-negotiable position. This technique is most appropriate when you have a fairly good idea of how the problem should be solved but are open to other potentially better solutions.

THAT'S FAIR

A widow approached Ibn Saud (King of Saudi Arabia from 1932 to 1953) and sought the death sentence for the man who fell on her husband and killed him. Being king, he could have given his verdict one way or another without any discussion. But he decided to engage the woman in consultation. He asked her whether the fall was intentional. She confirmed that the fall was accidental. Yet she was bent upon revenge. Ibn Saud tried to reason with her that accepting monetary compensation would be better for her than insisting on the man's death. After all it was an accident. She was adamant; she said it was her right to demand the death sentence for the man who caused her husband's death.

'All right,' said Ibn Saud. 'I accept your right to this man's life. But I shall decide how he should die. Take this man and tie him to a palm tree. Then you climb up that tree and fall on him. That will be fair because you can take away his life exactly the same way as he took away your husband's life.'

There was a long silence. The king broke it by saying, 'Perhaps you would like to take the money?' She took the money and went away. Being a party to the discussion, there was little she could do at this point other than accepting the king's suggestion.

Source: Adapted from an anecdote at http://www.anecdotage.com/index.php?aid=10692 (last accessed on July 16, 2010).

In spite of the risk involved, consultation is very useful, especially when the target's wholehearted collaboration is essential for execution. The beauty of this technique is that once the target contributes to the formulation of the solution, you can expect full support. There is an additional advantage. If you manage the consultation process appropriately, you may end up with a better quality course of action than you had planned.

Using Inductive and Deductive Reasoning

Using inductive and deductive reasoning is not really a persuasive move but rather a means to sustain all the moves we have identified above. It is difficult to imagine any persuasion attempt that does not use reasoning in some form or the other. Whether you depend on ethos or pathos for persuasion, the content of your communication consists largely of inductive or deductive reasoning. In fact, the target's mind has to accept the logic of your proposal for him to be persuaded. Ethos and pathos facilitate the process by either softening resistance or by dulling the mind so that it does not raise uncomfortable questions. We have already seen that exclusive reliance on logical reasoning will not result in persuasion because the mind can always question some aspect or another of your proposal and hold out.

Let us assume, for example, that you want to leverage your authority to persuade a subordinate or peer to accept your proposal. Let us also assume that what you ask him to do is not quite in line with the organization's current rules. You will obviously give him a reason why he must do it. You may show that it benefits the organization although it appears to violate some norms. Or, you may explain to him why it will benefit both him and you, and why that is acceptable. (This is possibly where you might introduce 'safety in numbers'—everyone else is doing it, so why not us?) The target may not question your reasoning if he accepts your authority infused with legitimate, expert, or referent power. He may trust your judgement and believe that although he has difficulty understanding your reasoning, you know better and so he should comply.

FRAMING

Framing is the heart of persuasion. It refers to the way a compliance request is presented to the target. It virtually determines whether a persuasive attempt will succeed or not.

One of Mahatma Gandhi's sayings aptly describes framing: 'There are people in the world so hungry, that God cannot appear to them except in the form of bread.' If a man is starving, food is the only thing he is receptive to. If he is thirsty, he will push aside even the most delicious food and reach out for plain water. This applies equally to persuasion. You have to understand what the target values and frame your message to match it. That is when your target will be receptive to persuasion.

We all look for things that benefit us. This is instinctive. If what's-in-it-for-me is one of our fundamental concerns, a message that shows how the action recommended is aligned with what we value and will benefit us, is framed appropriately; it has a very high chance of being persuasive. Young men, for example, are persuaded to buy deodorants that promise to make them attractive to women. The advertisements work because their framing matches one of the central concerns of young men.

There are bosses who enjoy micromanaging; there are other bosses who hate being consulted by their subordinates on every little issue. Some managers are proud of belonging to large and well-known companies; some others feel suffocated in them and enjoy working with start-ups. Some enjoy travelling and meeting new people; for some others travel is a pain. It is obvious that a compliance request that does not take into account such priorities and predilections of the target, will have hardly any persuasive power, irrespective of what techniques are employed.

In the following chapters we shall explore framing in greater detail.

CONCLUSION

In this chapter we have dealt with the basics of persuasion. We have noted the three persuasion factors identified by Aristotle: ethos, pathos, and logos. Of these three, ethos or the persuader's character is the most important. A target's resistance often melts away when faced with a persuader who is highly regarded and is powerful. Although, logos, that is, logical reasoning, appears in some form or the other in all attempts at persuasion, appeal to emotions is equally important for persuasion everywhere including the workplace. Even flawless reasoning with an abundance of evidence is likely to fail if the mind is not prepared through pathos and ethos.

Persuasive strategy consists of choosing the right mixture of persuasion factors through moves such as making oneself likeable, leveraging authority, creating indebtedness, stroking the target's ego, playing on herd instinct, getting small commitments, appealing to shared values, and engaging the target in consultation. Framing the compliance request in a way that matches the target's needs, values, and beliefs is extremely important for the success of persuasive attempts.

LESSONS LEARNT

▶ A combination of expertise and trustworthiness is a great asset for managers who want to be persuasive; positional authority enhances it further.

▶ While all persuasion attempts involve some reasoning, emotions play a critical role in disposing the target favourably towards compliance requests even at the workplace.

▶ From among several persuasion moves available, a smart manager chooses the most appropriate for the occasion as not all of them work in all contexts.

▶ Whether a persuasion attempt succeeds or not depends almost always upon whether the compliance request is framed in a way that matches the target's needs, values, and beliefs.

In the first two chapters we examined the manager's need for becoming persuasive, the three factors that underlie all persuasion, and the most common persuasion moves. In the next few chapters we shall take up specific contexts and explore the best ways of attempting persuasion.

REFERENCES

Adams, J.S. (1965). 'Inequity in Social Exchange'. In Berkowitz, L. (ed.), *Advances in Experimental Social Psychology*, Vol. 2, New York: Academic Press, pp. 267–99.

Burgoon, J.K., J.E. Dunbar, and C. Segrin. (2002). 'Non-Verbal influence'. In Dillard J.P. and Pfau M. (ed) *The Persuasion Handbook: Developments in Theory and Practice.* pp. 445–73.

Cialdini, R.B. (1993). *Influence: The Psychology of Persuasion.* New York: Quill William Morrow.

Cialdini, R.B. (2001). 'Harnessing the Science of Persuasion'. *Harvard Business Review*, pp. 72–9.

Kennedy, G.A. (1991). *Aristotle on Rhetoric: A Theory of Civic Discourse.* New York: OUP.

Kipnis, D., S.M. Schmidt, C. Swaffin-Smith, and I. Wilkinson (1984). 'Patterns of Managerial Influence: Shotgun Managers, Tacticians, and Bystanders'. *Organizational Dynamics*, Winter 1984, 0112: 3, pp. 58–67.

McCormack, M.H. (1986). *What They Don't Teach you at Harvard Business School: Notes from a Street-Smart Executive.* Toronto: Bantam Books.

Nayar, Vineet (2010). 'A Maverick CEO Explains How he Persuaded his Team to Leap into The Future'. *Harvard Business Review South Asia*, June 2010, pp. 94-97

Rhoads, K.V.L. and R.B. Cialdini (2002). 'The Business of Influence: Principles that Lead to Success in Commercial Settings'. In J.P. Dillard and M. Pfau, (eds), *The Persuasion Handbook: Developments in Theory and Practice.* Thousand Oaks: Sage.

Yukl, G. and J.B. Tracey (1992). 'Consequences of Influence Tactics Used with Subordinates, Peers, and the Boss'. *Journal of Applied Psychology*, 77(4), pp. 525–35.

3

The Persuasive Boss

INTRODUCTION

In this chapter we focus on becoming a persuasive boss. Managing subordinates is extremely challenging because in spite of common traits that draw them to work in a particular organization or a particular department, they can differ widely among themselves, especially in values, attitudes, and expectations. You cannot treat everyone alike as if they were sheep. At the same time, you will face resentment if you apply different norms for different individuals. If you want to thrive as a boss and get your subordinates to do what you want them to, you must invest in persuasive strategies because the formal power your organization gives you along with your position does not guarantee your subordinates' compliance.

Before planning to persuade your subordinates, you need to assess your strengths and limitations as a boss. At the very minimum, you have legitimate authority with associated coercive and reward power. Fortunately, subordinates generally respect it. But that is inadequate. You should also develop soft power over your subordinates by displaying a high level of professional competence along with moral character expressed through fairness, credibility, and trustworthiness. Your limitations include your being part of a system that severely limits your authority and freedom, irrespective of the level at which you operate.

In the latter part of the chapter we move on to the first-person account of a manager in a telecom company. She describes how her boss persuaded her to take up additional responsibility, which she had originally decided not to accept. When we analyse the incident, we discover that the boss used the following persuasive moves:

- ▶ Re-framing
- ▶ Emotional appeal
- ▶ Ego-stroking
- ▶ Appeal to shared values
- ▶ Being likeable and dependable

We also argue that if you want to be an effective boss, it is unwise to rely on short-term persuasion tactics. Your best bet lies in taking a long-term strategic approach towards persuading your subordinates especially by strengthening your credibility.

THE CHALLENGE OF BEING A BOSS

Of all your workplace relationships, the one with your subordinates appears to be the easiest to manage because your organization gives you formal authority over them. The higher your position, the greater your authority, and the larger your turf. But you will find the relationship with subordinates the most problematic and the hardest to manage even in the best of organizations. While you tend to have just one boss to manage, you will typically need to manage several subordinates. The trouble is that they may display bewildering variations in competence, motivation, values, attitudes, expectations, and willingness to accept your supervision. Some of your immediate subordinates may think you are too dumb to be their boss and challenge you indirectly or even directly in public. Some may be a thorn in your flesh. You have to forge these disparate individuals into a team and make it work smoothly to achieve your targets.

If you are a boss, you can think of yourself as a farmer; you have to plough your land by yoking together a bullock, a buffalo, a donkey, and a horse. That they are all tied to the same yoke and that you hold the handle does not guarantee control. They may pull you in different directions and stop you from ploughing. It matters little whether you are the owner–president of a company or a petty supervisor. As Shakespeare's Henry IV said, 'Uneasy lies the head that wears a crown.'

When you are in charge and have power, you may be tempted to flaunt it to get things done before you invest sufficiently in other options. But soon you will discover that it won't take you very far. Subordinates expect to be consulted and be a party to decisions rather than just executors of directives handed down to them.

Your subordinates should experience your formal power the way they feel the gravitational pull of the earth, that is, they don't feel it at all. They should be able to go about their life without being made aware of your power except when, as in the case of gravity, they defy the rules. In fact, authors Amar, Hentrich, and Hlupic provide evidence in a *Harvard Business Review* article (December, 2009), to show that managers who go easy on authority when dealing with subordinates are likely to be better leaders.

Your calculations go wrong almost routinely. A key member of the team ups and leaves in the middle of a project. Non-arrival of critical supplies stops urgent production. A major fire in an adjacent office block upsets everything in the neighbourhood.

An ego clash between two talented managers holds up a prestigious project. A team member's spouse commits suicide…Crises have a way of springing up at unexpected places at unexpected times and in unexpected forms. Subordinates happily throw the ball in your direction. It's your job to make sure that it doesn't hit the ground. You have to pass the ball on to someone else, but no one may be willing to take it. Yet you are accountable for your team's performance.

If routine management is tough, managing change is much tougher. You may have to change the way your team works. This is because the world around the organization changes and the team needs to adapt to it. People, however, tend to balk at change because, as Richard Hooker, the sixteenth-century Anglican theologian observed insightfully, 'Change is not made without inconvenience, even from worse to better.' Many things well beyond your control affect your team's work and make it difficult for it to achieve the preset goals. You have to get your subordinates to change to deal effectively with changing times. If you fail, you will not be an effective boss. You can, of course, give excuses for your failure, but if you are a whiner, don't expect to reach the top rungs of the corporate ladder.

You need to assess your strengths and limitations as a boss to figure out how best to get your team to do what you want. As we shall see later, you will also need to analyse the strengths and weaknesses of your team members before you can finalize a strategy.

YOUR STRENGTHS AS A BOSS

As a boss, the minimum asset you have is authority over your subordinates. You may possess other assets that include greater knowledge and experience than your subordinates and soft power. Let us look at each of them.

Authority

Whatever rung in the hierarchy you perch on, you hold power delegated to you by your organization. The range of power you wield depends on the position you occupy. If you are the CEO, for example, you have power delegated to you by the board, which ultimately derives its power from the shareholders who own the company. Because you are at the apex of the pyramid, you have direct power over your reportees such as vice-presidents and general managers, and indirect power over everyone else in the organization. The whole organization recognizes this equation. If you are an assistant manager, you have the same power delegated to you, but it is severely limited and diluted. You may be able to exercise it only on a few support staff. If a subordinate ignores it, there is little you can do other than an appeal to a higher authority.

In all cultures, people defer to authority. Right from childhood we are trained to comply with requests from people who hold authority. Initially, the authority figures are parents and other adults in the family. Later, the set expands to include teachers, doctors, priests, traffic police, and so on. We learn to comply with the wishes of all these adults. They use rewards and punishments to ensure obedience. The rewards offered by parents may be words of praise, food, gifts, or permissions. Parental punishments include scolding, inflicting physical pain, delaying food, and withholding privileges such as watching TV. Research shows that rewards are generally more powerful than punishments for ensuring compliance.

The colour and shape of rewards and punishments change as we grow older and move into the bigger world, but they always accompany legitimate authority and strengthen its compliance power. Like the Pavlovian dogs that salivate at the ring of a bell even after the food is withdrawn, we continue to submit to authority even when rewards and punishments are not projected prominently along with compliance requests.

One of the dimensions of the power derived from the position you occupy is your access to even more powerful people in the hierarchy compared to your subordinates. At higher levels in the organization, your position may give you access to powerful people in other organizations including the government. Such connections and the implied influence (ability to put in a word in favour of or against someone) also enhance your ability to get compliance from your subordinates. The simple reason is that this extends your ability to give out rewards and punishments in an indirect way.

This universal respect for authority is an important strength you have when you are a boss. When you ask your subordinates to do something that is legitimate, part of the contract, part of the tradition, and so on, you can generally expect compliance even when you have nothing other than your positional authority to base it upon. Your subordinates will not hold out unless they have an excellent reason why they need not comply.

The respect for authority is such that people listen to you and follow you if you speak authoritatively and decisively even when you have no authority. Assume, for example, that you are a motorist involved in a traffic jam. Everyone waits in their cars hoping that the traffic police will come to their rescue and somehow clear the jam. As the jam gets worse, if you get out of your car and direct the traffic confidently, the other motorists will meekly follow your directions.

Superior Competence, Experience

If you are a standard boss in a typical organization, you are likely to be older, more experienced, more management savvy, or more knowledgeable than your subordinates. It is rare that a boss is superior to all his subordinates in all areas. Because of the explosion of knowledge and universal accessibility to it, even bosses who start out with an edge over subordinates in technical knowledge may lose it quickly. This is well understood. You may be a young college dropout, but you may be able to have people more experienced, more managerially competent, and more knowledgeable than you as your willing subordinates if you have a brilliant idea, as Bill Gates and Steve Jobs have demonstrated. Similarly, if you have a few million dollars to invest, you may be able to hire people who are older, more experienced, more competent, and more knowledgeable than you. The idea is that there is at least one aspect in which you are superior to your subordinates. This superiority generates in them some respect for you, which in turn gives you power over them. You may be able to get their compliance because of this power.

Among all these attributes, managerial savviness is the most prized because it is the rarest. An MBA degree from the world's best business school doesn't give it to you any more than training in versification makes you a Kalidasa or Kipling. Irrespective of the level of your education and experience, you will be able to climb the corporate ladder quickly only if you are known to manage people in a way that you get the best out of them. Or, you can create and develop an organization of your own as Dhirubhai Ambani did with the Reliance empire. It is well known that he started out with very little formal education and even less money. But he had a rare talent for spotting opportunities and taking bold risks. He also knew how to get the best out of a wide array of people: employees, customers, shareholders, journalists, government officials, and regulatory bodies. It is not surprising that he was widely admired as an entrepreneur and feared as a competitor although he had his share of detractors.

Moral Superiority

In a letter to Bishop Mandell Creighton in 1887, British historian Lord Acton stated, 'Power tends to corrupt, and absolute power corrupts absolutely.' History confirms this insight. Few people ever get absolute power. Even with limited power people can become corrupt. They become overly self-centred and promote their own interests at the expense of others. In other words, they become blatantly unfair to others as they focus their efforts narrowly on serving themselves and abuse the power delegated to them.

Besides being competent, if you are scrupulously fair, credible, and trustworthy—a person of moral character, in Aristotle's words—and if you lead by example, you will enjoy enviable soft power over your subordinates. They will look up to you, and will be positively disposed towards complying with your requests. Here, we are referring really to referent power (Chapter 1). This moral authority is something you have to build up on your own; no one can delegate it to you. As you try to build it, you will discover that credibility and trustworthiness are extremely difficult to develop and time-consuming. You may face some opposition from your own bosses who may not like your uprightness. They may find your firm commitment to certain values uncomfortable, but they are bound to respect it. The fact that your bosses respect you helps your subordinates appreciate and accept your moral authority. If, however, your moral superiority is not accompanied by managerial competence, you may be treated as a well-meaning fool and your requests may not carry any persuasive power.

A GENTLE RAP

In 1996, I was Assistant Administrative Officer at the LIC (Life Insurance Corporation of India) Branch at Bareilly. I used to get to work every day by 9:45 am.

One day I started earlier than usual from home because I needed to go to a cooking gas agency's office on my way to work. For some reason that office was closed. So I went straight to my branch and reached by 9:30 am.

As I entered my floor, I saw a stranger cleaning and dusting. I asked him why he was doing it. He said that Ashok Johri asked him to do it. On being questioned further, he said that Ashok paid him Rs 25 a month for cleaning and dusting, and that Ashok had promised to give him more floors to clean for additional cash. I was surprised because Ashok was the employee who was supposed to do this job as well as provide all the officers with drinking water. I didn't say anything to the stranger.

About ten minutes later Ashok came in. By then the stranger had disappeared. Ashok saw me sitting in my office. He was a little surprised but he went on with his work, and brought me water. I asked him to meet me at 5 pm, that is, immediately after the office closed. He was puzzled. He asked me if there was anything the matter. I said no.

By 5 pm everyone had left the office apart from Ashok and me. I said I needed his advice. He thought I was joking. He asked, nervously, 'Who am I to give you advice?' 'You are the right person,' I said, and continued: 'I don't want to come to work from tomorrow. I would like to hire someone who will do my job for me. I will show him how to sign my cheques and do the other work I generally do. I'll pay him Rs 500 or 600 per month. Meanwhile I can save my salary and do some other business that brings me additional cash. What do you think of this plan?'

'That's not possible, Sir,' said Ashok. 'No one else can come in and work in your place, Sir.'

'But I saw a stranger doing your job here this morning.'

First he said he didn't know anyone coming in to do his job. But later he admitted that he had sub-contracted the job to a man so that he could do a lucrative job elsewhere. He apologized, and promised never to give me any cause for criticism. I said to him that I would forget about all this. I also added that if he did a good job, the Corporation would promote him in due course to the position of a clerk.

To my surprise and relief Ashok started doing his work conscientiously. Fortunately, the Corporation promoted him the following year. He was delighted. A few years later, when he retired, he narrated this incident in his farewell speech. He also thanked me for showing him the right path.

Source: As narrated by Mr T.R. Misra, Faculty Member, LIC of India.

YOUR LIMITATIONS AS A BOSS

While being the boss increases your persuasive power when the targets are your subordinates, there are also limitations that you need to factor in. The first limitation is that you are not free to do what you wish. You have performance goals and responsibilities, but never enough power to execute your agenda through your subordinates. Of course, you have authority over your subordinates. But as we have seen above, that authority does not ensure compliance. If several subordinates unite and ignore your instructions, or sabotage your projects, there is little you can do. Not even a king can rule if the majority of the ordinary subjects in his kingdom revolt against him. Similarly, subordinates are not bonded labour; they can walk out on you anytime. This is especially true in an open, liberalized economy. If several talented subordinates walk out, you will develop a reputation for being a bad boss, a boss who cannot manage talent. Such a reputation can stunt the growth of your career.

ARROGANCE OF POWER

President Lyndon B. Johnson (LBJ) was upset that his old friend, Senator William Fulbright criticized his Vietnam policy and warned against his 'arrogance of power.' Seeing Fulbright during a diplomatic reception in May 1966, LBJ pulled out a pencilled note from his housekeeper, Zephyr Wright. He stopped Fulbright, showed him the note, and said: 'Listen. You can hardly accuse a man of arrogance of power if his cook can write him this.' Then he read the note aloud: 'Mister President, you have been my boss for a number of years and you always tell me you want to lose weight, and yet you never do very much to help yourself. Now I'm going to be your boss for a change. Eat what I put in front of you and don't ask for any more and don't complain.'

Source: Paul F. Boller's *Presidential Anecdotes*, p. 323.

The second limitation is that you are part of a complex system. You have one or more bosses, and several peers. Your organization has a certain culture. You may have innovative ideas and energy; but some bosses and peers may not want to see you gallop away. They could be jealous or genuinely alarmed at the way you lead your team. They could put hurdles in your way in the guise of politically correct insistence on cost-effectiveness or more research before action. Together, they could strangle your dreams. If, for instance, you want to charge your customers for reusable carry-away bags and contribute that money to organized efforts at reducing pollution, as IKEA does, your boss or colleagues could stall it by arguing that you are not getting your customers to reduce their share of pollution but actually helping them absolve themselves of their responsibility by letting them pay for the pollution they cause. Their argument is unexceptionable, but their real objection may not be to your idea but to your leadership. Similarly, because of lack of support from the top you may find yourself unable to fulfil some of the promises to your team members. If you let your team down, you can't expect them to hold you on their shoulders.

You may have an additional handicap if you are an 'outsider': a woman in a male-dominated organization or a member of a minority (linguistic, religious, social, or political) in an organization populated heavily by members of the respective majority. You may find a huge wall of prejudices stopping you from reaching out to your subordinates. Sociologists have noted the Catch-22 situation or 'double-bind' women bosses are in. If they behave naturally, they are dubbed as too soft to be able to manage. As Judith G. Oakley says, 'The typical double-bind for women in leadership positions is that they must be tough and authoritative (like men) to be taken seriously, but they will be perceived as "bitches" if they act too aggressively.' Similar challenges confront bosses who belong to a minority in a majority-controlled organization.

THE BOSS AS PERSUADER

Keeping in mind the main strengths and limitations of a boss, let us analyse the way Tej Nirmal tried to persuade Lata Nair, one of the several managers reporting to him. Here is the background.

Tej was the department head with the Indian operations of a multinational telecom company. Ajit Kumar (name changed), one of the managers reporting to him, left the company in a huff after bungling a couple of important accounts. As the market was highly competitive, Tej had to find someone to step in immediately and take care of those accounts. This meant giving those accounts as an additional responsibility to one of his managers. He knew that every one of them would be right to turn down his request because they were all completely loaded with their own assignments. He also knew that assigning the extra work to any one of them without their willing acceptance would be counter-productive. He zeroed in on Lata Nair and tried to persuade her.

Here is Lata Nair's account:

Ajit's departure was quite sudden. He had messed up a couple of accounts, one very badly; so none of the colleagues were shocked except for the suddenness. Someone would have to step in quickly to fill the gap. The hot topic of discussion among several of us managers was on whose head the boss would dump the mess. Everyone said roughly the same thing: 'There's no way I am going to step in if the boss asks me. My hands are full.'

I don't know if the boss approached any of my colleagues. But he certainly called me and said he would like me to take on most of Ajit's responsibility, especially the two troublesome accounts. I was expecting such a request, and so I was ready with my answer. I said it was with great difficulty that I was keeping my head above water; I was sorry but there was absolutely no way I could take up any additional responsibility.

He appeared surprised, even upset by my response because in the past I had never said such an abrupt, emphatic 'No' to any of his requests. Obviously, he hadn't expected from me anything other than a cheerful 'Sure, Sir.' He said he was upset by my response because he never thought I would let him down in such a difficult situation. Then he asked me why I said no. Here is roughly how the rest of the conversation between us went:

Me: I'm already carrying a heavier burden than I should. Because of that many aspects of my life are suffering. Taking on additional responsibility would mean that I become a robot that just does the company's work. In any case, why me? There are several others. Why don't you ask one of them?

Boss: You know very well, Lata that you're the only one I trust in an emergency. If I were you, I would feel flattered that my boss held me in such high regard and trusted my competence.

Me: But I am unable to develop other skills and to devote enough time to my family.

Boss: You are a people-person, Lata. No one else I know in this office can manage an emergency like you. I remember vividly how you set right two rather messy things in the past. We must deal with the two accounts Ajit messed up. Losing them would be a severe blow to the company. We would look pathetic in the VP's eyes.

Me: If I take up additional responsibility, will you give me additional resources?

Boss: Certainly. You can ask me for any reasonable resources to do the job well, and I will make sure you get them. Think of your career implications. This is how you go up the ladder. You are proving yourself to the top management that you a capable and ready for higher responsibilities. And remember, you should delegate some of your routine work to your assistant so that you can focus on what only you can do.

Me: Let me think about it.

Boss: Sure, Lata. Let me know by EOD.

I returned to my office and thought about it. I increasingly felt that it was not a bad idea to take on the additional responsibility although I knew this would make life harder for me. But I have to put up with the pain that growth brings me. Saying no to this request might in effect be saying no to my growth.

As I thought more and more about the implications and recalled the boss's reassurance about giving me additional resources, I felt that the right decision would be to say yes to the boss's request. In the past he had never gone back on any of his promises. So I met him in the afternoon and told him I would give it a try. He thanked me and added that I had taken a wise decision.

Source: As narrated by Lata Nair. Her company's name has been withheld.

BOSS'S PERSUASIVE STRATEGY

We can readily see the unfolding of a coherent persuasive strategy in this successful downward persuasion attempt narrated by the subordinate. In her account, Lata may appear to be an easy, naïve target of persuasion. But it is based on Tej's reading of Lata's strengths, weaknesses, and expectations. He has correctly identified at least the following characteristics in her personality: she is keen on career growth, capable of hard work, non-assertive, somewhat sentimental, proud of being a people-person, and committed to the company. He has also correctly judged that she trusts him. After all he has always kept his word and been good and fair to her in the past.

We find several persuasive moves in the way Tej gets Lata to accept the additional assignment. We shall analyse them. We shall start with framing, which has a remarkable impact on the persuadee.

Re-framing

The discussion among the managers points to the way they frame the issue: the boss would want to dump the mess on one of them. Naturally, no one is interested in taking it. They should avoid it. It should be easy to refuse the boss's request with a clear conscience because everyone has an excellent excuse for not taking on the additional work.

Tej changes the framing completely during his discussion with Lata: 'This is how you go up the ladder. You are proving yourself to the top management that you are capable and ready for higher responsibilities.' For a young woman with ambitious career goals, this change in framing makes all the difference. She can see that it is in her interest to take up the additional responsibility although it will make her life difficult. She gets the right answer to the fundamental question every persuadee asks: 'What is in it for me?' The new assignment is no longer a dead weight that she has to carry, but a small ladder that will help her go up. It is especially attractive now because the boss has offered additional resources. Besides, by accepting the additional assignment she is also making Tej obliged to her. She is bailing him out of a tight corner. Someday, she will be able to use this credit when she needs a favour from him. Thus, the additional responsibility appears desirable because it will help her with her professional growth and enhance her influence on her boss.

Emotional Appeal

Tej starts his persuasion attempt with a direct, assertive request. He expects a positive response from Lata because she has, in the past, been generally receptive to his requests. If there is such a history, the boss may not need any elaborate persuasion strategies. Here, of course, Tej's move fails, and he's taken aback by Lata's clear, quick, and negative response.

TEJ NIRMAL'S PERSUASIVE STRATEGY

Tej Nirmal employs the following persuasive moves to soften Lata Nair's resistance and to persuade her to accept additional responsibilities.

Lata says that Tej 'appeared surprised, even upset.' It takes a lot of courage to say no to a request from the boss. It is perhaps harder for Lata because she has been saying yes to Tej's requests all along. She will feel hesitant and almost guilty about turning down a request from him. He deepens her sense of guilt by saying that she is letting him down in a difficult situation, that is, in a situation where he has no one else to turn to. There is no anger, no criticism, just pain. It is generally simple to counter anger and criticism because life is full of grey areas and we can always find some excuse for not doing a job well. But when the other person says that he is pained or upset by our behaviour, it is difficult to counter it. We have to do something to compensate for the pain we have caused. Accepting his request is an excellent way to do so. Tej is clearly targeting Lata's emotions. It works because of their excellent interpersonal relationship.

Stroking the Target's Ego

Having shaken Lata's resolve to avoid the assignment by appealing to her sense of guilt, Tej makes the next persuasive move: he strokes her ego. Responding to her half-hearted resistance, represented by her question, 'Why me,' Tej says: 'You're the only one I trust in an emergency.' Coming as it does from the boss, it is indeed high praise. He can trust any of her peers to do a good job under normal circumstances. But *not* in an emergency. To reinforce the value of his praise, he adds that *he* would feel flattered if *his* boss held *him* in such high regard and trusted his competence.

Even as this deepens her sense of guilt at letting him down, Tej goes on to praise her further: 'You are a people-person, Lata. No one else I know in this office can manage an emergency like you.' This could have been empty flattery, but it is not. He proves the genuineness of his praise by referring to two specific instances: 'I remember vividly how you set right two messy things in the past.' Tej has probably realized that Lata is quite proud of being a people-person and her achievements in managing people. She must also welcome his assertion that she's the one he looks up to in difficult times.

Tej's two-pronged approach—deepening her sense of guilt on the one hand and kindling her self-esteem on the other—breaches her wall of defence.

Appealing to Shared Values

Tej tops off his persuasive attempt with an appeal to their shared pride in the company. He mentions two specific outcomes, one of which will be painful to anyone who loves the company and the other painful to anyone who works in his office: 'Losing (the two accounts) would be a severe blow to the company. We would look pathetic in the VP's eyes.' On its own this may not have much persuasive power. Lata could respond by saying, 'Yes, you're right; please find someone who will rescue the accounts.' But in this particular sequence of events, the reference to collective pride in the company and loyalty to the specific office comes after Lata's resistance has been virtually removed. And, therefore, this appeal carries significant persuasive weight.

Making Oneself Likeable and Dependable

Tej also says and does things that make Lata like him. Apart from offering her more resources for doing the additional job well, he offers her a piece of friendly advice about delegation. She should delegate the routine stuff to her assistants, and focus on what she alone can do well. This reassures her that she will not be overwhelmed by the additional responsibility. It also gives her valuable directions on how to achieve more on her way to the top. This demonstrates to her Tej's interest in her welfare and growth rather than just his desire to get the job done. This adds to his soft power and raises him to the position of a mentor in Lata's eyes.

Also, Tej treats Lata with respect. He doesn't rush her into taking a decision right away. When she says that she would like to think it over, he gives her time till the end of the day. This is an excellent persuasive move. If she is pressured into saying yes on the spot, later she may feel trapped by her own promise, and as a result, she may not commit herself fully to the new project. By giving her time to think about the proposal after disposing her mind and heart favourably towards it, Tej is helping her buy his idea with full conviction. If new concerns crop up when she analyses the pros and cons or discusses them with a colleague, she can get back to Tej. We can say that she is taking this decision on her own; she doesn't feel that she is being persuaded to do something against her will although, when she came in, she was clearly opposed to taking on the additional responsibility.

Two more things are worth noting in Lata's account: Tej's trustworthiness and his confirmation that Lata has taken a wise decision. Tej has promised additional resources. Can she trust him? Suppose she says yes on the basis of his verbal promise, and then he drags his feet? She will be stuck. She doesn't have that worry, however, because 'in the past he never went back on any of his promises.' That she can trust him makes it easier for her to be persuaded by him. She believes that he will not let her down.

When Lata goes back to Tej to tell him that she will take on the additional responsibility, he thanks her but quickly adds that she has taken a wise decision. While it is a good idea to thank Lata, if Tej goes overboard with expressions of gratitude, it can make her wonder if she has been conned into the additional assignment. Tej's statement that Lata has taken a wise decision helps her confirm that the reason she accepted the request, career growth, is valid. She feels happy that she has taken this decision. At no point does Tej rely on or take recourse to his positional power as Lata's superior.

In a discussion on this event, Tej Nirmal said that he had not worked out any specific persuasive strategy in advance when he approached Lata with his request. He added that the persuasion techniques in the account were adopted spontaneously. He also said that he didn't praise people enthusiastically; as a result, when he did praise anyone, it was effective because it was accepted as genuine. He stressed the power of trustworthiness and credibility and identified them as the key to being a persuasive manager.

LONG-TERM STRATEGIES VERSUS SHORT-TERM TACTICS

There are highly effective short term persuasion tactics. Successful salespeople are very good at using them. In his *Psychology of*

Persuasion, Robert Cialdini cites many examples of such tactics. When, for example, a real estate agent shows you first an attractive house with an inflated price and then another attractive house with a high price, you may choose the second one because you find it reasonable (although the price is well above its real market value). The agent does not force you to buy the second house. The first house with the inflated price is set up merely to create the contrast that persuades you to choose the second one. You are essentially tricked into willingly paying a lot more than the second house is worth.

Another favourite tactic is an artificial creation of scarcity or at least an impression of scarcity. As Cialdini observes, we have a tendency to buy up what we believe will be in short supply not because we need it but because we believe there will be an imminent shortage and we're worried we may not get it when we look for it. Scarcity enhances value. When the time available to take a decision is limited, as in a discount sale open for just one day, we may not even critically evaluate our needs. We buy first—we don't want to miss what we believe to be a great bargain—and think, perhaps regret, later.

Such short-term tactics are inappropriate in a long-term relationship between a boss and subordinates. If a subordinate realizes that she has been tricked into making a commitment, she will lose trust in the boss. She will be extra sceptical when she deals with him next. She may withhold cooperation even when the boss's requests are reasonable.

> The most important persuasion tool you have in your entire arsenal is integrity.
>
> —*Zig Zigler*

If then, you are a boss, your best bet lies in taking a long-term strategic approach towards persuading your subordinates. You need to develop trustworthiness and enhance your credibility on multiple fronts. Any persuasion tactics or techniques you use should be backed by a well-earned reputation for fairness and integrity.

CONCLUSION

We have seen that managing subordinates is extremely challenging because they differ widely among themselves, especially in values, attitudes, and expectations. Although you have formal power delegated to you by your organization, you cannot always depend on it to ensure compliance from your subordinates. This is true irrespective of how high your position is in the company's hierarchy. This is true in spite of the respect we generally feel for authority. It is true notwithstanding the coercive and reward power that nearly always accompanies formal authority. The way forward, then, is to keep your formal power in the background and to rely on persuasive strategies to get your subordinates to do what you want.

LESSONS LEARNT

▶ While people, in general, respect authority, you cannot depend on it to get their whole-hearted compliance.
▶ A persuasive strategy consists of a coherent combination of various persuasive tactics and moves.
▶ Appropriate framing of the issue is critically important to persuasion attempts.

- ▶ In an organization, it is unwise to depend on short-term persuasive tactics of the kind salespeople use with one-off customers—subordinates who feel that they have been conned into compliance are likely to quietly dilute their commitment.
- ▶ Smart managers enhance their professional competence and strengthen their credibility and trustworthiness. This gives them highly effective soft power which makes their subordinates receptive to their ideas and proposals.

You will find that without taking your peers into confidence, you may not be able to achieve many of your targets. The additional challenge posed by your peers is that you have no formal power over them. In the next chapter we shall examine ways of persuading your peers to do what you want them to.

REFERENCES

Amar, A.D., C. Hentrich, and V. Hlupic (December, 2009). 'To be a Better Leader, Give Up Authority'. *Harvard Business Review*, 87(12), pp. 22–4.

Boller, P.F. (1996). *Presidential Anecdotes*, New York: Oxford University Press.

Oakley, J.G. (2000). 'Gender-based Barriers to Senior Management Positions: Understanding the Scarcity of Female CEOs'. *Journal of Business Ethics*, Vol. 27, pp. 321–34.

4

The Persuasive Subordinate

INTRODUCTION

In *The Effective Executive*, Peter Drucker says that one of the surest signs that a manager is effective is that he manages his boss well. The effective subordinate, says Drucker, does not toady up to his boss but starts out with what is right and presents it in a form that is accessible to the superior. This is the quintessence of upward influencing. If you ignore this and focus exclusively on managing your subordinates, you will severely limit your career growth.

You must influence policies at the higher levels for the sake of your company because managers at the top may not understand the ground reality the way you do. If you are able to influence policies at higher levels, your standing in the eyes of your subordinates will rise. It, in turn, will give you more persuasive power in your dealings with your bosses, and will accelerate upward climb.

Your main strength as a subordinate is that your bosses cannot achieve their goals without depending on you. If you want to influence your bosses leveraging their dependence on you, you need to understand their strengths and weaknesses on the one hand and your own strengths and weaknesses on the other.

The persuasion techniques available to you as a subordinate are limited because you have a smaller powerbase than your boss. Here are the most common techniques available to you:

- ▶ Logical reasoning
- ▶ Ego-stroking
- ▶ Consultation
- ▶ Crowd support

What techniques you should choose depends on your boss's personality and management style, your personality and style, the organizational culture, and, of course, the nature of the issue at hand. You are likely to be most persuasive when you combine different techniques as part of a coherent strategy. The key to persuasion, however, is appropriate framing of the issue. That may determine whether you get a hearing or not.

IMPORTANCE OF UPWARD-INFLUENCING SKILLS

Abdul Farhat joined InterFin Systems four months ago as Senior Manager of Training. He has always enjoyed conducting training sessions on soft skills. His training has been received very well by the participants of these workshops. He believes that he has been able to touch the lives of at least a few individuals, especially software managers, and has made a difference to the way they look at life and manage it. At InterFin Systems, with about 450 software engineers and chartered accountants working on financial services products, he does not get any opportunity to teach. His responsibility is to identify experts in a variety of relevant technical fields and soft skills, and organize their training programmes. He sat in on a couple of soft-skills programmes he helped organize and was convinced that he could do a better job than some of these excessively paid experts.

During his conversations with some of the senior colleagues, he realized that a few of them might be interested in conducting a couple of sessions in their areas of expertise once in a while although they were inundated with work. They also said that this would lead to greater bonding among the employees.

The managing director, however, is firmly convinced that the company's core competence is developing financial products and that everyone should focus on that. She wants all services including training to be outsourced so that the company gets the best in the country. Abdul, however, believes that while focusing on the company's core competence is excellent, there is no harm in allowing a few interested individuals to contribute voluntarily to the company's training programmes rather than depend exclusively on external trainers. The MD dismissed the idea when Abdul casually mentioned the possibility to her a fortnight ago. Should he now make a special attempt to persuade her to change her mind? Or should he put up with his role as a mere organizer of training programmes? How should he go about persuading the MD if he believes that his proposal will benefit not only himself but also the company?

For you to be a significant contributor to your organization's growth, it is not enough that you follow all the directives from the top sincerely and competently. While that is certainly required, it is equally important that you influence policies at levels that are higher than yours. In your regular interactions with your peers, subordinates, and, perhaps, external agencies, you become aware of the ground realities in a way that people at higher levels may not be. Your encounter with the market may give you fresh ideas that your organization can exploit before the competition does. You should be able to share your ideas with your bosses and get them to review some policies which you believe need changing. If you fail to play this critical role in your organization, you are not a 'complete manager.' Similarly, if the top brass of your organization shields itself against being influenced by managers at lower levels, it will deny itself critical inputs and die.

If you are unable to influence policies at higher levels even after you present your ideas and suggestions to your bosses, you may feel frustrated. You may not put your heart and soul into the implementation of the policies that are handed down to you from the top. You may simply do the bare minimum required to get by. There are instances where managers appear to comply but actually sabotage initiatives from the top because their views, which they believe are superior to the official one, have not been taken seriously. Such developments are not good either for you or for your organization. But perhaps the fault lies in the way you present your views to those who matter. Or the timing may be wrong. You must master the techniques of influencing your superiors so that your organization benefits from your insights, and your own climb up the corporate ladder is fast.

There is another important reason why you should strive to influence your bosses favourably. If you can get your bosses to do what you want, your standing in the eyes of your peers and subordinates becomes enhanced. Your soft power over them grows tremendously because if you are seen to influence your bosses favourably, you tend to become an informal leader among your peers, and you will be able to get many things done by them and for them. This, in turn, makes your bosses treat you with respect and accept your proposals because you have become an important ally for the top management. We can see here a strong virtuous cycle emerging.

If you are talked about in your organization in connection with successful upward-influencing attempts, your visibility increases. Greater visibility attracts challenging assignments within the company, which give you an opportunity to showcase your talent. This not only adds to your soft power but also makes your promotions appear well deserved and free from distracting controversies. Another consequence of increased visibility is that head-hunters will begin noticing you. They may open up an entirely new world of opportunities for you.

Yet another advantage of refining your upward-influencing skills is that it enhances your persuasive skills in general. When you try to persuade your bosses, you don't have either coercive or reward power to support your attempts. But if you manage to be persuasive in such situations, it should become easier for you to persuade others when you have the support of coercive or reward power.

YOUR STRENGTHS AND LIMITATIONS AS A SUBORDINATE

In a *Harvard Business Review* classic, 'Managing Your Boss,' originally published in 1980, authors John J. Gabarro and John P. Kotter highlight the interdependence between subordinates and bosses. Your dependence on your boss may be greater than her dependence on you to achieve the organizational goals. But the fact is that bosses cannot function efficiently nor achieve anything significant except by standing on the shoulders of their subordinates. This dependence is at the root of your power over your bosses.

If you want to use this power to influence your boss's decision-making, you need to understand your boss and yourself, say John J. Gabarro and John P. Kotter, echoing Drucker's advice in *The Effective Executive*. They say that you should understand your boss's goals and pressures, strengths and weaknesses, organizational and personal objectives, blind spots, and preferred style of working.

Understanding the target is the key to appropriate framing of issues and choice of persuasion techniques. Well laid-out rational arguments supported by compelling evidence may, for example, be wasted on an authoritarian boss who may, however, be susceptible to well-delivered flattery.

Equally important is your self-knowledge. You must be clear about your needs, strengths and weaknesses, and preferred style of working. You may not be able to convert the boss to your style of working; so you should identify any major irritants in your relationship with him and at least tone them down for you to have a reasonable chance of winning him over. But never sacrifice your backbone at the boss's altar!

Your ability to walk out is a strength and one of your limited sources of power over your boss, if you have worked yourself into a profile that makes you highly valuable in your organization or department. You may be able to have your way with a reluctant but weak boss if you threaten to quit. A strong boss may, however, let you entertain the impression that you are indispensable, but call your bluff if you actually put in your papers. A strong boss may reckon that even if your resignation causes an upheaval, he will be able to find a replacement; he may prefer it to constantly being subjected to the threat of resignation. Once you resign, you may also discover that you were not as indispensable as you and others thought you were and that your organization or your department didn't collapse at your departure. Therefore, threatening to quit is not a particularly praiseworthy persuasive move when you deal with your bosses. You should generally prefer your other strengths as the base for your upward-influencing attempts.

A FINANCIAL CONTROLLER REVOLTS

I am a chartered accountant. In December 1996 I joined a big trading and contracting company in Doha, Qatar. This was my first overseas job.

Three things hit me hard as I took charge of the company's Finance and Accounting department. First, the financial controller I was supposed to replace had already left. So I had no one to guide me other than the three Egyptian clerical staff in the accounts office. Second, the books of accounts were all in Arabic, a language that I couldn't make head or tail of. Third, the accounts were maintained manually. I learned that the process of issuing an invoice typically took about a month if everyone put in extra time!

I asked the top management to let me computerize the accounts. They readily agreed in principle. In fact, their suppliers of machinery, spare parts, and consumable stores, who were mostly from Western Europe, had implemented ERP. They asked me to find out about the cost of computerization.

I supplied all the information within days. They said they would give me a decision in a day or two. I announced in the office that from January 1, 1997, we would computerize accounts. I stopped them from opening any manual book of accounts. We waited till January 7. There was no action from the MD. I was intrigued by the delay in decision-making. On enquiry I found that they had made a half-hearted attempt at computerization earlier in the year and then abandoned it. Although manual book-keeping was time-consuming and error-prone, the top management was quite comfortable with it. They were in control. Computerization, which they did not understand at all, made them apprehensive. They were worried that the office staff might indulge in irregularities that they wouldn't be able to detect. I also discovered that the sales department, dominated by Egyptians, did not want computerization, either. They were all happy with manual account keeping in Arabic.

It was January 15. There was no response yet from the top management about computerization. There was panic in the accounts office because vouchers were piling up but no books had been opened. They were following my instruction not to enter any transaction except in a computer.

On January 15, I repeated my request to the MD. He said that they were still making up their minds and that in the meantime I should organize manual bookkeeping, as in the past. I felt I had to act decisively now. 'Please approve computerization right now,' I said firmly. 'If you still insist on manual accounts, I will be better off taking my flight back to New Delhi.'

I was surprised at what I had blurted out. After all here was a job that paid me, tax free, four times as much as my old job in India. Should I throw it away on an issue like this? But the threat worked like magic. He asked for a meeting with the company that would computerize our accounts. I introduced him to a software company manned by Arabic-speaking Jordanians. They explained to him, in Arabic, the implications and the advantages. He gave the go-ahead. I, however, decided to enter the computerization gradually. I got my assistant manager, also a chartered accountant, to do all the entries for January 1997. It was not his job, but I wanted the system to be up and running without any error to avoid giving the staff or the MD an excuse for going back to manual bookkeeping.

Source: As narrated by Sanjeev Kumar Gupta, FCA, General Manager— Finance, Neuerth Group, Dubai.

Your true strength as a subordinate lies in your expertise for which you have been hired. No one else in the organization may understand as deeply as you do the people and things you manage. This, however, also acts as a limitation because someone else can be trained to do your job as well as you do, perhaps better. If you are a woman manager interested in climbing to the higher rungs of the office hierarchy, you may encounter additional hurdles. You need to identify your strengths and weaknesses in the context of your organization in order to plan your upward-influencing moves satisfactorily.

SUBORDINATES' CHOICE OF PERSUASION TECHNIQUES

You may use any technique or combination of techniques and succeed in persuading a particular boss to do something in a particular situation. But the realistic range of techniques available to you as a subordinate is limited because your power-base is smaller than your boss's. The smaller your power, the narrower is your choice of persuasion techniques.

Of course, there is nothing fixed about how best you can persuade your boss to do what you want. But there are certain factors—such as the power distance between you and your boss, the boss's personality and management style, the organizational culture, your strengths, weaknesses and personality—that determine the efficacy of your attempts to persuade. Taking these determinants into consideration, you should, like a tactician, arrive at the most promising mix of techniques.

Determinant 1: Power Distance

The power distance between you and your boss could depend on your position in the hierarchy or the degree of the boss's dependence on you. If, for example, you are an assistant manager in a large company, the distance to the managing director is so long that protocol may not even let you communicate with him directly; you may have to send him a letter or e-mail through the channel determined by the company. There is no guarantee that he will even read your letter or e-mail. Someone else may very well dispose of it on his behalf. If, however, you are a personal assistant to the same managing director, the hierarchical power distance is longer but your job gives you easy access and you may be able to use flattery or personal appeal to persuade him to do what you want. As you may be privy to information that may damage his reputation, you will have far greater power over him than merited by your position in the hierarchy.

The personal assistants of some powerful politicians are occasionally in the news for the clout they wield merely because of their proximity and easy access to the leaders. It may not be very different in many large and hierarchical companies. When you attempt to persuade managers several rungs above yours, you will do well to take into account the roles played by such gatekeepers in your organization. Alternatively, you could first persuade someone who has direct or easy access to the top boss.

Determinant 2: Boss's Personality and Management Style

The boss's management style determines to a great extent the range of persuasion techniques you can successfully employ. Research by Daniel M. Cable and Timothy A. Judge shows that managers who report to a transformational boss are more likely to appeal to his values and vision rather than use hard strategies such as pressure to influence his decision-making. They may also use consultation as a means of involving him in their projects and getting his support. If the boss is unresponsive to reasoning or value-based appeals, subordinates may quote rules and precedents or approval by higher authorities to persuade him. This makes sense because persuasion works best when there is a match between what the target is looking for and what the agent is offering.

If your boss is not impressed either by your performance or your potential, your direct attempts to persuade him may fail irrespective of the techniques and tactics you use. This is to be expected because, as we have seen in Chapter 2, a great deal of your persuasive power comes from your 'ethos.' If your credibility is low, your reasoning and appeal to emotions will not evoke in the boss the kind of response you expect based on the strength of your evidence. In such cases, it is wise to choose an appropriate intermediary. If you can impress someone who has the boss's ear, you may be able to influence your boss through them (see box below, The Way to a Boss's Heart). This is not unlike what a less favoured child in a family does when he wants something from his parents. He approaches them through his sibling who is in their good books, and it nearly always works.

THE WAY TO A BOSS'S HEART

A few years ago I worked as the brand manager for a medium-sized company that sells its products (stationery) all over India. It was driven by the owner, who was the managing director. I reported to him.

It was difficult to work with him because he would change his mind frequently and without any notice. Nobody could figure out what he would approve and what he would not. So I started observing him. I soon realized that there were only two people in the company he consistently listened to: the sales director, who was in the corporate office in Mumbai, and the production director, who was in the plant in a big town in Maharashtra. What was common between them? Both these were his younger brothers.

I took the initiative in meeting the sales director frequently. I bounced many ideas off him over lunch or coffee in the corporate office. I gradually noticed two things. First, the managing director started treating my ideas with greater respect. I guess he had been hearing good things about me from the sales director. Secondly, he started approving all my proposals that I had run past the sales director. Again, I guess the MD approved my proposal after checking with the sales director. Because I had already run them past him, his response must have been positive always.

Source: As narrated by Ritesh Mohan, currently Marketing Manager of a major retail company in one of the Emirates.

Determinant 3: Your Personality

Your personality may restrict the techniques you choose to persuade your boss. If you are an extrovert, for example, you may attempt to persuade the boss not by logical reasoning but by personal appeal after praising him to make him feel good. If you are an introvert, you might cringe at having to resort to this and will avoid it if you can. If you enjoy confrontation, you might like to bring pressure on the boss to accept your proposal. And again, if confrontation makes you uncomfortable, you are likely to rely heavily on rational persuasion.

Your special strengths may have a bearing on the persuasive techniques you adopt. You may, for example, be excellent at writing analytical reports leading to crisp recommendations. It will not be surprising if you depend on written reports as the main means of persuading your boss. If you believe that you can present your proposals most forcefully when you speak, you are likely to choose presentations and one-on-one discussions when you want to persuade your boss. *But your success will depend on your ability to match your technique with the boss's preferred style.* As Drucker reminds us in *The Effective Executive*, it is generally a waste of time to talk to a 'reader' and equally wasteful to submit a longish report to a 'listener.'

Reluctance to adapt one's style to the boss's expectations can lead to many disappointments. This may be the main reason why women generally get lower compensation than men at the same level. Shellye Archambeau, who has been running major businesses at IBM and Blockbuster and is currently the CEO of software company MetricStream Inc, says, '...many males on my team would stop by and have a conversation with me about their financial needs and expectations. Throughout my career I only had one woman actually come and talk about her financial needs during raise time. When people came, it was the men.' Male and female bosses perhaps expect to be asked for a raise, and men ask. Women hope that their good work will be noticed and rewarded accordingly. They don't blow their horns, and aren't heard.

Determinant 4: Regional Culture

Your regional culture and organizational culture may shape the broad contours of upward-influencing strategies that are likely to succeed at your workplace. If you are a manager in a heavily rule-driven organization, your upward-influence tactics may emphasize that rules are being scrupulously followed. Similarly, in a high power-distance culture (in which people accept highly unequal distribution of power), access to the top management may be difficult; managers may then be forced to use indirect means. Although rational persuasion is the most widely practised upward influencing tactic, some researchers have found that Chinese managers do not welcome it because it can lead to open disagreement, which they want to avoid at all costs.

After studying the effects of gender and power on upward influence, Julie O'Neill concludes that gender, on its own, has little impact on the choice of influence tactics by subordinates, but power does. The impression that women subordinates have a smaller range of persuasion tactics than their male counterparts, says O'Neill, stems from the general observation that women tend to be in positions with less power. If they are in positions of power, they will have the same range of persuasive techniques as their male counterparts when they persuade their bosses.

The upshot of all this is that there is nothing rigid about the best way to persuade your boss to do what you want. The right choice of techniques depends on the power distance between you and your boss, the boss's personality and management style, the organizational culture, your strengths and weaknesses, your personality, and the nature of the issue at hand.

MOST COMMON TECHNIQUES

Influence researchers, especially David Kipnis, Gary Yukl, and their associates, have identified the following as the most common persuasion tactics used by subordinates to persuade their bosses: logical reasoning, ingratiation, consultation, and coalition. We shall examine each of them briefly. These, except coalition, were introduced in Chapter 2.

Logical Reasoning

In response to a deep fall in sales caused by the recession, the MD of Zenith Meditroniks decides to cut costs aggressively. One of the first measures he contemplates is a drastic reduction in air travel by managers in sales. He believes that replacing it with train travel would lead to big savings. Two of his senior managers try to dissuade him from going ahead with this plan. Dilip Kumar argues that people used to travelling by air would find it annoying to switch to the train and that they would lose motivation to work hard for the company. The MD dismisses this argument saying that people would understand that these are difficult times. Karan Sastry proves to the MD with the help of numbers that although rail fares are significantly lower than air fares, the overall savings will be negligible when the loss in productivity during the long hours spent in rail journeys is factored in. The MD realizes that trying to be penny-wise might make him pound-foolish and modifies the plan to replace all air travel with rail travel.

Several researchers reporting from different parts of the world and across industries confirm that logical reasoning with the support of factual evidence is the most commonly used persuasive move in upward-influencing attempts. Bernard Keys and Thomas Case, for example, support it in their article, 'How to Become an Influential Manager.' Deepti Bhatnagar's study of managers of an Indian bank shows that they found logical reasoning to be the most appropriate and effective tool in upward-influencing efforts.

There are two main reasons why logic has become the subordinates' favourite tool to influence decisions by their bosses.

▶ In the unequal power relationship with the boss it gives the subordinate at least the illusion of a level-playing field. Logic is logic whether it comes from a temporary typist or the managing director. There is no shame associated with surrender to reason and factual evidence. Of course, we have already seen that logic doesn't deserve the killer reputation it enjoys. A boss can question most inductive and deductive conclusions if he doesn't want to accept them. But logic gives you a shot at success when you have no godfather to hold your hand.

▶ It is safe for the boss to accept a well-supported proposal. A managing director cannot say that he acquired a start-up at a premium because it belonged to his son-in-law, even if that is the truth. He has to show that he acquired the start-up at a premium because the strategic fit between it and the company would lead to substantial profits. Thus, when a boss finds that a subordinate has provided good reasons to justify the decision, he can accept the proposal confidently.

Ego-stroking

When you stroke your boss's ego, you put him in a good mood by praising him, agreeing with him perhaps on a controversial decision he has taken, offering him support in a risky initiative, or doing something that he likes. It is difficult for most people not to be pleased by the good things others say about them. Some people are more easily pleased than others. Praise is so soothing that some people are pleased even when they know they don't deserve it. The good mood so created dulls the mind or weakens any resistance it may have to the proposal being made. At times, however, the proposal is presented soon after compliments are delivered; at times there is a perceptible gap in time. Absence of a gap may make some bosses suspect that the words of praise are not genuine. If they do, praise loses its power to influence.

As we have already noted, praise has an ugly cousin, flattery. If you are a manager with some self-esteem, you will not want to use flattery to get what you want from your boss. If you indulge in sycophancy to achieve your goals, you will demean yourself. But becoming hypercritical of your boss and withholding praise even when everyone else believes that he deserves it is different. It reflects a small mind, not a genius. It may also indicate your inability to understand what it means to be a boss.

If the gap between you and your boss is great, neither your praise nor your criticism may mean anything to him. He is likely to ignore it. If, however, that gap is narrow, the impact of both can be significant. Your best bet may be to combine criticism with praise: criticism for what he has failed to do well and praise for whatever he has done well. It raises the value of your praise tremendously in the eyes of your boss. Your reputation in the organization for being fair and independent will grow too. That should help you in your professional growth.

GETTING AROUND THE BOSS

I am the Marketing Manager of a large retail company based in Kuwait with operations in many countries in the Arab world. I report to the General Manager, a British expat. He reports to the Executive Director, a Pakistani who has grown the seventeen-year-old company from day one. He reports to the owner, a Kuwaiti. The owner's son has been recently inducted into a position almost equivalent to that of the ED. The owner likes the ED and trusts his judgement almost blindly. The owner's son likes the GM, and supports him. Both the GM and I have been with the company for less than a year. I must also say that the ED often asks me for things directly; I guess the GM resents this, but can't do anything about it because of the ED's clout. I also approach the ED occasionally because once he signs a document no one asks any questions.

Recently, I wanted to get into an agreement with a widely circulated newspaper for a gift-voucher scheme. The readers of the paper would enter certain competitions organized by it; the winners would get our gift vouchers from the newspaper. They would bring the vouchers to our retail outlets and get our goods in exchange. In return, we would get free advertising space in the newspaper. In other words, we wouldn't need to pay the newspaper anything. As our gross margin was 55 percent, we would be spending only 4.5 dinars on every 10-dinar voucher that was redeemed. My expectation was that the free vouchers would bring many shoppers into our retail outlets. I was sure many of them would buy more products than what they would get in exchange of the vouchers. I thought this was a great scheme because there was no cash outflow while we got publicity and an excellent chance to sell additional products.

When I presented the idea to the GM, he turned it down. He felt that the free voucher scheme would hurt our brand image because people didn't attach any value to what was given away free. My arguments in favour of the scheme fell on deaf ears.

I went to the ED and explained the scheme to him. He liked it instantly. I was sure he would because in the short period that I was at this company I had been observing him. He liked any promotional idea that did not involve substantial cash outflow. Once he bought the idea, I asked him to send me an e-mail, with a copy to the GM, giving me his approval. He did.

The GM was furious. He asked me why I went to the ED when he (the GM) had already said no to the proposal. I apologized to him profusely. Then I said my team and I wanted the idea to reach the ears of the ED. As he liked it very much, there was little I needed to do.

The GM cooled down. We get along well now.

Source: As narrated by an Indian marketing manager working in Kuwait; all names have been masked or dropped at his request.

Consultation

As we have seen in Chapter 2, consultation is a process of involving the target in dealing with a problem. It has two advantages when it is used to influence your boss. First, it almost eliminates resistance because it is not perceived as an act of persuasion. You invite your boss to help you solve a problem. If her solution does not match your requirement, you can point out the difficulties associated with it. She will either suggest ways of dealing with them or be open to your suggestions. Deftly handled, the process of consultation can be a powerful tool for persuading your boss. The second advantage is that buy-in is complete; you can expect full support from the boss for the solution you have arrived at in consultation with her because she part-owns it.

As a means of persuasion, consultation has some drawbacks too. A clever boss may be able to see through your plan and take you far away from your agenda if she does not like your idea. Once you consult the boss, you cannot ignore her suggestions without giving adequate reasons. If you fail to, you may be stuck with a solution that you don't want. Besides, some bosses may not like to spare time for such consultations. If you run to them repeatedly seeking advice on problems you should be solving, you may end up annoying rather than pleasing them. So consultation is a technique that you should use sparingly when attempting to persuade your boss. It should ideally be attempted in areas in which she considers herself to be an expert. Then you will be able to create a powerful combination of consultation with careful ego-stroking.

Crowd support

When you find that you are unable to persuade your boss on your own either because your reasons are not overwhelming or because your power-base is too small, you may take the help of others. This is the heart of crowd support or coalition as a persuasion technique. The manifestation of this technique could be as innocuous as letting the boss know that there are several others who hold the same view as you. If several people think like you, your view must be respected and your request granted. In this technique, you buttress your view with the strength of numbers. This generally works because most bosses wouldn't want to alienate several people by going against their view.

At the other extreme of the same persuasion technique is collective pressure. Here you let the boss know not only that there are several others who agree with your point of view but also that they are willing to withdraw their support to him if he doesn't agree to your proposal. A common manifestation of this technique is the threat of industrial strikes held out by the office bearers of workers' unions. On their own, the office bearers of a union have no coercive or reward power over the management. However, when their proposals have the support of the majority of the union members, they acquire it and their persuasive efforts become more fruitful.

STRATEGIC COMBINATION OF TECHNIQUES

Here is how one of the managers studied by Bernard Keys and Thomas Case narrated his successful attempt to persuade his superior, a vice president, to sanction construction of additional space:

> I wanted to convince my immediate superior that the current facilities were inadequate for the current volume of business; I also wanted to impress on him that the current facilities were too small to support our efforts to increase our market share in a rapidly growing area. First, I got him to visit the branch several times when the branch was particularly busy. With the help of Accounting, I regularly provided statistical reports on overall

growth in the area, the way our competitors were growing, and the way our market share was going up. I then invited him to a meeting of several of our customers and prospects; I had called that meeting to let him know the kind of potential business in the area. While all this was going on, I worked hard to increase all levels of business at the branch. I also encouraged some of my key customers in the bank to say good things about my branch when they met my senior managers. Eventually my superior bought my proposal; we built an addition to the building which allowed me to hire several new employees. (Summarized from Bernard Keys and Thomas Case, 'How to be an Influential Manager.' pp. 45–6.)

This manager's strategy consists of a coherent arrangement of different techniques and persistence. His core technique, however, is logical reasoning: the company can grow its business profitably if the branch has additional accommodation. What is noteworthy is his attempt at providing graphic supporting evidence for his claim that there is plenty of business waiting in the wings and that his branch is ready to grab it. The boss had no idea that the evidence, which appeared natural, was, in a sense, manufactured. There is no cheating or fake data, but the vice-president got a rosier picture of the business prospects than warranted and bought the subordinate's idea.

The branch manager succeeded in selling his proposal because he organized the environment in such a way that the vice-president perceived his proposal not just as reasonable but as essential to deal with the growth that he is generating. This is another manifestation of framing in persuasion attempts. Right framing, as we have already seen, is an essential condition for success in persuasion.

SMALL CHANGE, BIG GAIN

One day Mr Wang and his friend were walking along the road. Mr Wang went into a shop and bought a pack of cigarettes for 10 yuan.

When he tried to light a cigarette, he realized that he didn't have matches. So he went back to the shop. Finding that he had only a 100-yuan note and no loose change, he asked for a free box of matches (a box of matches cost just five cents). The shopkeeper, however, refused. He insisted on payment. Mr Wang was crestfallen. How mean of the trader! Wang returned to his friend and told him what happened. He said, 'don't worry, I'll get you a free box of matches.' He went to the shop, and asked for a pack of cigarettes, and asked for the price. He was told that it was 10 yuan, to which he replied that he wanted a discount. The shopkeeper refused. Then the man said he only wanted a tiny discount of five cents. Then the shopkeeper readily agreed. The man gave him a 10-yuan note; when the shopkeeper was looking for small change, the man said, don't bother; you can perhaps give me a box of matches instead of loose change. The shopkeeper readily obliged.

Source: G.O. Faure, (ed.), How People Negotiate: *Resolving Disputes in Different Cultures*, p. 51.

On its own a box of matches cannot be given away irrespective of the low price. But when its price, just five cents, is set against the price of a pack of cigarettes, 1,000 cents, it appears to be very small and insignificant. Framing makes a big difference to the way people accept or reject your requests.

CONCLUSION

If you want to be an effective and successful executive, it is not enough to manage your subordinates; you must learn to manage your boss. In a sense, it is your duty to influence your superiors because you are the eyes they see the world through. That they depend on you for a part of the business is the source of your strength and persuasive power. If you influence your superiors, simultaneously your power to influence your peers and subordinates also grows. They are unlikely to do what you want them to if you are an impotent whiner.

LESSONS LEARNT

▶ As your power base is smaller than your boss's, the range of persuasive tactics you can use is limited.
▶ The techniques that are generally most appropriate for upward-influencing are:

   ▶ Logical reasoning
   ▶ Ego-stroking
   ▶ Consultation
   ▶ Crowd support

▶ If you want to influence your boss's decision-making, you need to understand her strengths and weaknesses, her values, and her goals.
▶ Self-knowledge is equally important: you need to know what your strengths and weaknesses are within the context of your organization.
▶ A persuasive strategy that matches your boss's style and your personality is likely to be far more successful than what the reputation of different strategies may lead us to believe.
▶ You are likely to be most persuasive when you combine different techniques as part of a coherent strategy.
▶ The key to upward persuasion is appropriate framing of the request.

We have looked at downward and upward persuasion. It is time to move to lateral persuasion. In Chapter 5, we shall study persuasive strategies that work best with your peers.

REFERENCES

Bhatnagar, D. (1993). 'Evaluation of Managerial Influence Tactics: A Study of Indian Bank Managers'. *Journal of Managerial Psychology*, 8(1).

Cable, D.M. and T.A. Judge (2003). 'Managers' Upward Influence Tactic Strategies: The Role of Manager Personality and Supervisor Leadership Style'. *Journal of Organizational Behavior*, 24, pp. 197–214.

Drucker, P.F. (1967). *The Effective Executive.* London: Heinemann.

Farmer, S.M., J.M. Maslyn, D.B. Fedor, and J.S. Goodman (1997). 'Putting Upward Influence Strategies in Context'. *Journal of Organizational Behavior*, 18(1), pp. 17–42.

Faure, G.O. (ed) (2003). *How People Negotiate: Resolving Disputes in Different Cultures.* Dordrecht: Kluwer Academic Publishers.

Gabarro, J.J. and J.P. Kotter (2005). 'Managing Your Boss'. *Harvard Business Review*, 83(1), pp. 92–9.

Keys, B. and T. Case (1990). *How to Become an Influential Manager. The Executive*, 4(4), pp. 38–51.

Kipnis, D., S.M. Schmidt, C. Swaffin-Smith, I. Wilkinson (1984). 'Patterns of Managerial Influence: Shotgun Managers, Tacticians, and Bystanders'. *Organizational Dynamics*, 0112(3), pp. 58–67.

O'Neill, J. (2004). 'Effects of Gender and Power on PR Managers' Upward Influence'. *Journal of Managerial Issues*, 16(1), pp. 127–44.

Yukl, G. and J.B. Tracey (1992). 'Consequences of Influence Tactics Used With Subordinates, Peers, and the Boss'. *Journal of Applied Psychology*. 77(4), pp. 525–35.

5

The Persuasive Peer

INTRODUCTION

Persuading peers is arguably tougher than persuading bosses and subordinates because your peers may have no stake in your achievements. Logical reasoning with the support of factual evidence is expected in lateral persuasion, but it is rarely enough. Peer persuasion tends to take long and patience is essential for success. Ridiculing those who hold out can be counter-productive. Ability to persuade peers is a great asset because it enhances your influence over both your bosses and subordinates.

Personal example is probably the most powerful factor in persuading your peers to adopt what you propose. When your peers find that you derive many benefits from the practice you advocate, they will want them too, and adopt your method . Such peer influence can grow into peer pressure.

We have to learn to influence peers in groups. But it is unwise to trust even a well-crafted and well-delivered presentation to win your peers over. You will do well to practice the strategy of 'persuasion cascade' in which you persuade the opinion leaders one-on-one to accept your ideas. They can create a cascade of support which will eventually help you win the whole group over.

Influence researchers have identified the following techniques, apart from logical reasoning, that managers generally use in peer persuasion attempts:

- ▶ Ego-stroking
- ▶ Getting crowd support
- ▶ Bargaining and offering exchanges
- ▶ Making personal appeals
- ▶ Quoting rules and traditions
- ▶ Consulting and seeking advice

You will need a combination of two or more such techniques to be effective. But for them to succeed, you need to take a strategic, longterm approach to becoming persuasive. You should develop a reputation for expertise in some field where your peers can look up to you with respect. Such lateral leadership is important for your persuasion techniques to succeed. You should also increase your visibility through a variety of means. These include contributing useful and innovative ideas to meetings, perhaps maintaining a blog, and using social networks. Networking is essential if you want to be an influential peer.

THE CHALLENGE OF PEER PERSUASION

Among all the targets you have to persuade in your organization, your peers—especially your counterparts managing other functional areas—are probably the toughest. The reason is simple. They generally have little incentive to go along with your request. If you are a boss, you have a stake in what your subordinates are doing and how they are doing it. If you are a subordinate, you have a stake in what your boss is doing and how she's doing it.

This mutual dependence gives a boss power over her subordinates and vice versa. It is at the back of your mind when you try to persuade either your boss or your subordinates. It is also clear to both you and your persuadees that you are the boss or that you are a subordinate.

When you try to persuade your peers to do their bit of work in time or in a particular way for you to meet your personal or organizational goals, some may not go along because it may not make any difference to them whether you succeed or not. Their schedules and priorities might be different and their hands may be full. Or perhaps your progress *does* matter to them. If you race ahead, they may appear to be laggards by comparison. They might want you to slow down. Or their contributions to the organization may be evaluated differently from yours and, therefore, they may have no incentive in helping you improve your performance.

Some of your peers may hold out because being persuaded by you might be perceived as accepting your leadership. When everyone is trying to be the leader among equals, this is quite natural. Yet, you need to win them over if you want to climb to the top. The higher you go, the harder it is to achieve your organizational goals without involving your peers who manage other functional areas. You would look silly and incompetent if you kept running to the common boss complaining about lack of cooperation from your counterparts in other departments. If you want to be persuasive among your peers, you need to build up leadership and moral authority by developing expertise in some aspect or performing well above average.

LESSONS FROM A PEER PERSUADER

Here is an account of the way a new CFO tried to change certain inefficient but well-entrenched practices of his peers in a large manufacturing company.

It was Behram Sabawala's first review meeting after he joined Voltas Limited as the CFO of its Unitary Products Business Group. The Vice President (Operations) chaired the meeting. Divisional leadership was in attendance for a quarterly review of operations. Behram was surprised at the way the discussions went and the minutes were written. Everybody made speeches; the elaborate minutes captured virtually everything that was said. He realized that nobody ever went back to those voluminous narratives. In spite of the length, the minutes didn't state clearly who was supposed to do what. As a result, there was no real monitoring of the decisions taken.

Behram found this practice terribly wasteful. He suggested that the team move to simple, crisp, Excel-based (to prevent verbiage!) action-oriented, responsibility-fixing minutes in the format he had picked up from Boeing, a Baldrige Excellence Award winner. The minutes consisted of brief answers to just four questions:

- ▶ *What* needs to be done?
- ▶ *Why* should it be done?
- ▶ *Who* (name of a person, not a department) will do it?
- ▶ *When* (a specific date) will it be done?

If things did not go as planned, the managers responsible had to raise the red flag and explain why to their immediate boss or their team as soon as it became evident that they would miss the deadline. Corrective action would, if possible, be taken before it was reviewed by the committee at the next meeting.

A review of the 4W minutes would be the first item on the agenda of the next meeting. Each item was colour-coded. GREEN was for tasks that were completed as planned and did not need any further review; YELLOW pointed to tasks in progress; RED highlighted the tasks that were not completed and needed the committee's focused attention. Thus, there was specific follow-up and an ongoing review. There was accountability. Any member of the team—not just the bosses—could raise questions about why those responsible for certain actions did not carry them out.

Behram was surprised by his peers' resistance to this productive idea. Their attitude appeared to be somewhat like, 'Look, we've been around here for quite a while. We know how to run this business and how to monitor progress. We need to keep detailed minutes of the meetings so that in future we can return to them just in case we wanted to find out who held what views and why certain decisions were taken. They would also need to be produced at various audits and assessments as back-up to evidence reviews having taken place.' To Behram's chagrin, this view appeared well entrenched across the team.

As a newcomer, Behram did not have enough bandwidth to win his peers over. So he decided not to press them but to adopt the 4W system of minutes in his own division and demonstrate the gain in efficiency. As time went by and communication emerged a key challenge across the organization, he and his team also began tracking what came to be branded 'WWW'—What Went Well and What Went Wrong.

There was no overnight surge in support! However, when it became apparent at quarterly review meetings that one division was achieving breakthroughs across the system and the stringent review mechanism was identified as one of the principal causes, another CFO adopted the 4W approach to minutes writing and began similar regular reviews with his team. It took some time for this benchmarking to happen; but once it did, it spread quickly to other parts of the company.

Behram believes that today this stringency of follow-up and focused review is one of the chief contributors to his organization's success. Other companies in the Tata Group have also benefited

from it through the 'learning and sharing' provided by assessors as part of the Tata Business Excellence Model (TBEM) assessments.
Source: Based on a discussion with Behram R. Sabawala, CFO, UPBG & EPBG, Voltas Limited.

We can readily draw five lessons in persuasion from Behram's experience. First, it is not easy to persuade your peers to change their practice even when the advantages of the proposed change are so obvious to you that you can't imagine any of them not rushing to hug you in gratitude. Behram was surprised at his peers' resistance to his suggestion that they adopt the 4W approach to minutes writing. After all, the practice he recommended had an excellent pedigree: Behram had picked it up from Boeing, a winner of the Baldrige Excellence Award. He did not stand to gain anything personally if all divisions adopted the 4W model. The change would benefit them and the whole organization. Why then did they reject it without giving it a try, even though their meetings and minutes were undoubtedly wasteful? It appears that they did not want to change a well-established practice just because a newcomer found it wanting. Your arguments are unlikely to persuade your peers to change their well-entrenched practices. You can expect counter arguments when you propose something new.

Second, sarcasm and criticism are unlikely to be persuasive. Behram could have criticized his peers, at least behind their back, for being 'a bunch of bumbling idiots' and pontificated that the company had no future if it continued to behave so inefficiently as it did. He did not. Criticism and snide remarks would have alienated them and made it impossible to get their willing cooperation on any of his projects. He did not abandon his attempt to persuade them; neither did he run them down.

Public criticism of weak and even dependent peers is unlikely to lead to trouble-free compliance at any level. They will strike back in indirect and at times unpredictable ways. That is what the Americans learnt (see box below, A Puppet with a Mind of its Own) when they criticized Hamid Karzai, president of Afghanistan, in international media in an attempt to shame him into following the American agenda.

A PUPPET WITH A MIND OF ITS OWN

Hamid Karzai, president of Afghanistan, is an American puppet. He owes his presidency to the Americans. He depends on them for money and protection. This gave the American officials the impression that they could order him around; that there was no need to try persuasion. They chastised him in public and threatened tough action against him for not doing enough to root out corruption, one of the American demands.

All that changed in March 2010, according to *The New York Times* (April 9, 2010, 'U.S. Now Trying Softer Approach Toward Karzai'). Now the American administration officials are bending over backwards to please Karzai. President Obama sent him a 'respectful letter' thanking him for the dinner in Kabul. Secretary of State, Hillary Clinton, now tries to appeal to him as a 'fellow politician.'

The reason for the change of heart is simple, hints *The New York Times*. Tired of Western hectoring, President Hamid Karzai showed his defiance by hosting the President of Iran. He went on to state that he would consider joining the Taliban if Western criticism did not stop.

The Americans need just a puppet president to achieve their goals and withdraw their soldiers from the killing fields of Afghanistan. Karzai is indeed a puppet. They can oust him any day. But they can't get another puppet. They know it. Karzai knows it too.

The Karzai story demonstrates the limits even of a superpower when it has to deal with its peers.

Third, action persuades where arguments fail. Behram quietly carried out the change in his own division and demonstrated its impact on his division's performance. Even then there appears to have been a kind of denial, initially, on the part of his peers because they were sceptical of the value of the change he had proposed. As his division stood out from the others repeatedly, however, his suggestion could no longer be ignored. Once one fellow CFO adopted the 4W model being followed by Behram, there was a snowball effect. No one wanted to lose out. Although Behram was a newcomer and had no formal authority over the other CFOs, they started looking up to him once he demonstrated the visible impact of the adoption of his proposal on his division's performance. Gradually, he acquired informal leadership and moral authority among his peers.

Fourth, persuasion is rarely a one-shot affair, especially if the environment is challenging. Behram's peers took two years to accept and adopt his proposal. No single technique, however powerful, is likely to work. You may have to use different combinations of persuasive techniques over time to persuade your target. In Behram's case, rational arguments and supporting evidence from a respectable source such as Boeing did not work. It was the demonstration of the impact of his proposal over several quarters that did the trick.

Fifth, if you win your peers over, you will have the satisfaction not only of seeing your ideas adopted but also of feeling your visibility in the organization go up. You will be talked about favourably within the organization. Once your visibility goes up, new and challenging assignments are likely to come your way. They will further enhance your status and make you even more influential. Soon, people in other companies will also get to hear about you.

PEER PRESSURE AND PERSUASION

Your professional peers are also your jealous rivals. While they may dismiss your ideas initially, they will adopt them once they fear that they will lose out if they don't. Your success generates the pressure to conform. Kelly Hall, Executive Director of strategic planning at Partners Community Healthcare in Boston, writes in *Harvard Business Review South Asia*, that peer pressure can be superior to financial rewards in getting doctors to change some of their practices. She cites the example of her own organization in support. In it, peer pressure came from publication of comparative performance data that had been gathered and tabulated transparently. No one was exerting pressure on any peer, but all of them felt the pressure not to be outdone by their peers. Those who lagged behind felt obliged to find out the superior performers' techniques and to adopt them.

We have already noted that pressure and coercion can be counter-productive when it comes from the boss. Why should peer pressure be persuasive? The difference between coercion from the boss and peer pressure is that in the latter no one individual is pressuring anyone else. Everyone goes about their business. When you find that your peers are getting certain benefits—recognition, money, promotion, and so on—that elude you, there is pressure on you to adopt their practices so that you get them too. You may conveniently forget that you were highly critical of some of those practices initially. You may quietly adopt them, especially if you find several peers doing so. We can describe this pressure as self-administered. As a result, there is no resistance. This kind of peer pressure becomes very persuasive.

When you adopt a practice that you were once critical of, you may refine it and remove some of its weaknesses. This is similar to what companies routinely do. They imitate the valuable innovations of their competitors and often do better than the creators of the original. As Oded Shenkar shows in his book, *Copycats: How Smart Companies Use Imitation to Gain a Strategic Edge*, several well known global companies of today have been imitators rather than innovators. He says that Visa, MasterCard, and American Express imitated Diners Club, who pioneered plastic credit cards. McDonald's copied White Castle and Wal-Mart copied Corvette. Imitating peers and rivals is not flattery but a matter of survival.

We may find ourselves ignoring norms or lowering performance levels if we find our peers doing so. People who never bribe may, for example, start doing so if they find several people around them doing it. Interestingly, as Griskevicius et al. (2008) point out in their article, 'Applying (and Resisting) Peer Influence,' when dire public warnings are issued against those who violate certain rules, the rate of violation goes up, not down. Those who may never have thought of disobeying those rules get to know through those public warnings that a lot of people are actually disobeying them and getting away with it. That knowledge takes away the sting of the warning and prompts them to ignore those rules. Griskevicius et al. also observe that the number of hotel guests who reuse bath towels to reduce the burden on the environment goes up dramatically when an appeal for it is accompanied by the information that most guests reuse the towels. Thus, peer behaviour does influence people in different directions.

To demonstrate the persuasive power of peer behaviour, Griskevicius et al. cite the example of Sylvan Goldman who invented the shopping cart and introduced it in his stores in 1937. It was an excellent device that would make it easy for shoppers to buy as much as they wanted without getting tired or seeking others' help. But Goldman discovered that in spite of his repeated advertisements and explanations, he could not persuade his shoppers to use the wheeled carts. Men were reluctant because they thought they would appear effeminate if they pushed such carts instead of carrying their shopping. Women wouldn't touch them because the carts reminded them of prams. It was only a few elderly shoppers who took to them. That made the carts even less attractive to the majority of the shoppers. Then Goldman hit upon an idea. He hired several models, men and women, of different ages and asked them to wheel the carts in the store and shop. A young woman employee standing near the entrance told the regular shoppers, 'Look, everyone is using the carts. Why don't you?' That was the turning point. A few shills easily accomplished what logic, explanations, advertisements, and exhortations failed to do. Within a few weeks shoppers readily accepted those carts (visit http://realcartu.com/goldman/ for a detailed account).

Of course, peer pressure does not work on some very strong individuals. They may not want to be seen adopting practices initiated or promoted by their professional rivals. They may justify their own practices vigorously and cling to them or come up with better alternatives. Peer pressure works best when it is not perceived as deliberate. Even strong individuals may go along if they feel that they are doing something that they consider useful for themselves. It is when they perceive themselves as targets of persuasion that they do not respond to such pressures.

INFLUENCING PEERS IN GROUPS

Many managers overrate their credibility. They trust logic, evidence, and their own supposed credibility to persuade groups of peers to accept new ideas. They naïvely believe that a well structured and well delivered presentation will effortlessly sell their ideas. They may be successful if the issues involved are superficial or uncomplicated. But many issues are coloured by emotions such as fears and apprehensions. One or two vocal members of the audience can turn the tide against the presenter by arousing the audience's fears at times by referring to issues which have little to do with the theme of the presentation.

If you want to persuade a group to adopt something complex, you will do well to invest in a strategy that Bernard Caillaud and Jean Tirole call the 'persuasion cascade.' This strategy is driven by the power of peer influence. To create a persuasion cascade you release information selectively and sequentially to certain key members of the group before the final push. You get one member to accept your proposal. You then use his acceptance as the base for persuading another member to accept it. Or, you persuade one member to accept your idea and then get her to sell it to others in her circle of influence. You will do well to target, for the initial one-on-one persuasion, members who are likely to be somewhat critical. Once you have dealt with their concerns and they have accepted your proposal, they will lend tremendous credibility to your idea in the eyes of your peers.

The word lobbying is often used negatively in this context. There is nothing wrong with lobbying if it consists of personalized and serial attempts at persuasion ahead of public announcements and presentations. The advantage of these persuasion attempts away from the glare of publicity is that you can discuss issues without getting bogged down by irrelevant or unimportant details and grandstanding. It gives persuasion a chance. When managers find that several key members are in favour of a proposal, they refrain from arguing against it unless, of course, they feel very strongly against it. Lobbying becomes dirty when you pay for a person's or group's concurrence.

It is not always possible to meet key members of a group privately in advance of a public gathering. That makes it harder for you to persuade the group to accept your proposal. In such cases, you can increase your chances of winning the group over if you can show that your proposal is being practiced by similar individuals or organizations. This is because some group members tend to shoot down proposals by imagining all sorts of serious problems in implementation. A reference to successful implementation by comparable peers, individuals or organizations, helps in two ways. First it proves that the proposal is feasible. Second, the proposal gains persuasive power derived from peer influence.

PEER PERSUASION TECHNIQUES

Researchers have identified the following techniques as the most commonly used in influencing peers: ego-stroking, getting crowd support, bargaining, making personal appeals, quoting rules and traditions, and finally engaging the peer in consultation. We shall look at each separately but these techniques are rarely used in isolation. Generally, you will find a combination of two or more such techniques in successful acts of persuasion. The nature of the persuasion task, the time available, the nature and attitude of the peer(s), and your personality will determine the combinations most suitable for you and the persuasive strategy you should adopt.

Ego-stroking

Also called ingratiation, ego-stroking is found in different contexts and different relationships, as we have seen in the earlier chapters. There is a very good reason for its popularity. It is powerful. If done well, it is effective almost always because we like people who think well of us and agree with our ideas. We tend to treat their requests favourably. For ego-stroking to work, your persuasion target should believe that you mean what you say when you say good things about him. There are many ways of achieving this. You have to choose an approach that suits the target and the context. One approach is to separate praise from any specific persuasion attempt. Prefacing a request with even well-meant words of praise can be perceived as a ploy and discounted. Another way is to praise a person in public but when she is absent. When your words of praise are brought to her by a third party, they will be taken seriously and in the right spirit. Yet another highly recommended approach is to combine praise for certain aspects with criticism of certain other aspects of an achievement. This balance of praise and censure helps the peer take your comments seriously.

BRINGING PEOPLE ON BOARD

Pyramid Systems is a small company owned and run by a wife and husband team in London. The husband is the Managing Director. They have a group of five managers including an international marketing manager. An external consultant, I am invited to their quarterly management meetings, which are invariably run well and on time.

I went to Pyramid's board room last month to attend the quarterly management meeting. It was to start at 10 am. But three people were missing: the MD, his wife, and the international marketing manager. At 10.05 am the MD and his wife rushed in. They didn't appear to be their usual selves. I wondered if they had an argument. I asked them if they were okay. They said they were okay, but I wasn't sure. I asked them whether they would like me to step aside for a while. They reassured me that there was no need for that at all, and that it was time the meeting started. Yet they appeared disturbed. So I asked them, 'Can I help in any way?'

Then they came out with the reason for their loss of composure: their international marketing manager refused to attend the meeting. He was upset and said he was undervalued and made to feel like a failure.

'Would you like me to talk to him?' I was somewhat tentative because I was myself a little startled by the turn of events. The MD readily agreed to my suggestion.

I went over to the international marketing manager's office and met him there. 'What's the matter, John,' I asked him after exchanging the briefest of preliminary pleasantries. He had come to respect me and trust me because he had seen me contribute to the management meetings several times.

John burst into a litany of his woes: 'I feel like an absolute failure. I am unable to concentrate on anything. I tend to be slow in responding to e-mail. I travel so much I may miss some important e-mail when I go through my inbox at a busy airport...'

I listened patiently. Clearly he was under a lot of stress and was seeing everything in a negative light. A reality check was required! When he stopped, I asked him for specific examples when his peers or customers had complained to him about his style of working during the past few months. He said he couldn't recall any. Then I asked him if anyone had praised him for anything he had done during the few months. He said the MD had congratulated him on doing a difficult assignment very well.

As I asked him for specifics, he began to realize that failure was his perception; evidence pointed in the opposite direction. Once his failure perception was analysed and eliminated, he was much more relaxed and positive. He was more than willing to attend the management meeting.

For the first time in Pyramid's history the management meeting started late; but everyone including the international marketing manager contributed to the meeting wholeheartedly.

Peer Influence/Pressure

We have already looked at peer influence and peer pressure. Letting the target know that several people of her kind have adopted the position you advocate is using crowd support to enhance your persuasiveness. An extension of this technique is to hint that your bosses or others, who are highly regarded in the relevant community, also subscribe to the same position. Your credibility is essential for this technique to work unless you show solid evidence, such as published data, of the support you claim.

Bargaining

Exchange or bargaining is another common technique to get peers on board. You can offer them something that they value in return for giving you the support that you are seeking. This answers the question, what-is-in-it-for-me, in a way that satisfies them and induces them to support your position. You might make terrible mistakes if you don't make an effort to understand the peers' needs and value systems. Some may be looking for money, some for publicity, some for recognition, some for political support, and so on. If you offer money when he is looking for respect and recognition, the persuasion attempts may end in abject failure.

IN SEARCH OF RESPECT, FRIENDSHIP

In the opening scene of the film, *The Godfather*, Bonasera (a well-to-do Italian-American undertaker) meets Don Vito Corleone on his daughter's wedding day. Bonasera, a family friend of the Corleones, tells the Don that two young men had severely beaten up and disfigured his daughter who refused their advances, complains that the judge let the men go free, and asks him to have the two men killed in the interests of justice. He says, 'I'll give you anything you ask,' implying any sum of money. After all, the Don and his gangster family make money through crime.

Don Corleone spurns the money being offered; in fact, he is offended. He chides Bonasera for not speaking to him with respect, not coming to him in friendship, not calling him godfather.

Bonasera takes the hint, asks the Don to 'be my friend,' calls him godfather, and kisses his hand. Pleased, Don Corleone, accepts his request and tells the undertaker that one day he may ask for a service, but until then he (Bonasera) can take 'this justice as a gift on my daughter's wedding day.'

It is possible to engage in exchange without specifically offering anything in return while seeking the peers' support. That they can expect something in return is implied. They may not need anything now, but you will give them what they want when the time comes. This works well most of the time. We need to be aware, however, of the risks involved. They might ask for something, like Eklavya's right thumb, that can debilitate you financially, politically, or ethically. But once you are deeply indebted to them, you may find it difficult to wriggle out. Even if you manage to wriggle out, the unpaid debt may continue to haunt you.

Personal appeals

Personal appeals may work with peers who know you well, respect you, trust you, and admire you for the personal qualities you display. Several peers may support your initiative even if they don't think it is great. Their only reason may be that they don't want to disappoint you or appear disloyal to you. It is obvious that a personal appeal can work only if you have treated your peers with respect and generosity. When they respond favourably to your personal appeal, they are not looking for anything in return. They are paying back a fraction of what they have received from you.

When you rely on personal appeals, you should be aware of the risks involved. You may overestimate the worth of your favour. You may come away content from a persuasion attempt involving personal appeals to your peers, believing that you will get their support. On the crucial occasion when you expect it, however, it may not be forthcoming in spite of any promises you may have received. You may be like some parents who take decisions regarding their children without consulting them convinced that their children will do exactly as they tell them to. Those children may embarrass their parents publicly by defying them.

Quoting rules and traditions

Quoting rules and traditions is a surprisingly effective technique of persuading peers. Respect for authority that most of us feel is at the heart of this technique's success. Another reason for its effectiveness is that compliance with rules is the predominant employee behaviour. We may unwittingly violate some rules or sub-rules of our organization. If someone points out that we are violating a rule, we are likely to change our behaviour to be on safe ground. Quoting rules may not, however, work if we know the rule and the penalty for violating it and still break it. If the breakers of certain rules are generally law-abiding and have high credibility, they may be able to persuade others also to break those rules. They may be able to convince others, as Mahatma Gandhi did with his Civil Disobedience Movement, that those rules are unjust or have outlived their purpose.

Similarly, traditions are like unwritten rules. We follow them almost mindlessly. Traditions also reflect the vision of the organization that we are members of. If we have bought into the vision, we will be willing to change course to align ourselves with the tradition. Traditions are basically majority behaviour straddling the past and present. That generates peer pressure to conform. Reference to traditions may not work with some individuals who defy them because they no longer believe in them. As in the case of rule-breakers, those who defy certain traditions may be the bold innovators who may persuade the majority to swim against the tide.

Consulting peers

Consulting peers and seeking their suggestions are excellent ways of involving them and getting them to commit to certain things. It is for a good reason that consultation is widely used in upward, downward, and lateral persuasion. It strokes the target's ego because consulting someone is a way of showing them respect and telling them that you value their opinion. Any resistance they may have to your proposal comes out and is reviewed cooperatively rather than confrontationally.

We should be aware of the flipside of adopting consultation as a technique in lateral persuasion. While no peer expects you to follow every suggestion she makes, she may refuse to respond to your attempts to consult her if she finds that even after considerable discussion you do not carry out any of her suggestions. Consultation, therefore, may not be an appropriate technique if you are unwilling to make any changes in response to the suggestions the peers may make.

As in other directions of persuasion, logical reasoning is prominently present in lateral persuasion. When a proposal is backed by factual data and evidence, reasoning succeeds if other conditions, especially the persuader's credibility and the persuadee's receptivity, are conducive. Reasoning can fail spectacularly if those conditions are not favourable.

LONG-TERM STRATEGIES

For your peer-persuasion techniques to work, you need to develop certain long-term strategies. They consist essentially of an approach to life that shapes your behaviour towards your peers. We shall turn to them now.

Lateral Leadership

When you persuade your peers to do something that will help you reach your organizational goals, you are assuming a hint of lateral leadership. You may lose support from some quarters if you show off the power that comes from your lateral leadership. In such cases, it is a good idea to carry on lateral persuasion quietly, even indirectly.

In 'How to Become an Influential Manager', authors Bernard Keys and Thomas Case narrate the experience of a zone manager who supervised twenty-five stores in his zone. He initiated a very successful programme to handle defective merchandise. He wanted all the zone managers in the country (US) to adopt his programme. He was, however, apprehensive about how they would respond. So he asked his store managers to tell their counterparts in other zones about the programme and the sizeable savings that they were making. Those store managers shared the story with their zone managers, who, in turn, approached him for information and advice, and ultimately adopted the programme. What is remarkable in this incident is that although he persuaded his peers—the other zone managers—all over the country to adopt his innovation, none of them suspected that he had persuaded them. Trying to persuade them openly would have led to resistance, especially because of the leadership angle. We all know how easy it is to find fault with and reject any new programme.

This does not mean that you should make yourself invisible and work indirectly whenever you have to persuade your peers. On the contrary, you should develop a reputation for expertise in some field so that your peers look up to you at least in that aspect. It is because the zone manager did not have a reputation for any expertise that he chose the indirect approach. Now that several other zone managers consult him on how to reduce costs by adopting his programme, he has started building a reputation. Soon he will be able to recommend changes and improvements directly to his counterparts. And, not surprisingly, they will be more than willing to follow his recommendation.

Contributing useful and interesting ideas at the company meetings you attend is a sure way to establish lateral leadership quietly and gradually. Many managers waste this great opportunity by keeping their mouths shut during discussions. Some others attend meetings without any preparation. They talk a lot without saying anything. They don't establish any kind of leadership. All they manage to achieve is waste everyone's time.

Blogging on topics that you can claim some expertise in is a way in which you can establish lateral leadership on a larger scale. Your peers will visit your blog when they realize that they can gain insights from it. With more and more people visiting your blog, your visibility increases and along with this your ability to influence decision-making at different levels. As there is nothing official about blogging, your gain in authority and power is personal. It is not tied to the position you occupy or even the company you work with. The gain in informal authority enhances your persuasive power all around.

Successful blogging requires the ability to write interestingly and memorably. Unfortunately not every expert has this ability. If you are one of those who never enjoyed writing and would walk across the Sahara and meet people face to face rather than write, all is not lost. You may be able to hire a ghost-writer who can convert your expert comments into well-sequenced and readable weblogs.

Networking

If your proposal is extraordinarily attractive, your peers, who have never interacted with you, might adopt it enthusiastically on the basis of its strengths alone. But the chances are slim because few ideas are pure nectar. If you want to persuade peers, you will do well to be part of a network of managers who will help and support one another. A reasonably good working relationship with your peers is essential if you want their support in your initiatives. When you try to persuade someone within the network, you will still need to employ several techniques. The difference is that being part of the network, the target can be expected to be positively inclined towards you. When you are part of a network, you develop informal mutual dependence and indebtedness. Because of growing mutual dependence, even the most powerful members of a network will not be able to ride roughshod over the weaker members as the US discovered in its dealings with Kyrgyzstan and Ethiopia (see box, Weak-kneed America?). Every member of a network—whether an individual, organization, or country—acquires persuasive power. In a sense, this gives even the weakest members a level-playing field in a competitive world.

WEAK-KNEED AMERICA?

The US is proud of its democracy and its mission to make the world safe for democracy. In fact, its invasion of Iraq was justified partly on the fact that its ruler, Saddam Hussein, was a dictator and a violator of the human-rights of his own people. The US also happens to be the richest and the most powerful country on earth. Yet, it is unable to persuade the dictators ruling some of the poorest countries to adopt democracy. Kyrgyzstan and Ethiopia are excellent examples.

Kyrgyzstan (population 5 million) is probably the poorest country in Central Asia. Its president, Kurmanbek Bakiev, had been accused by human-rights groups of repressing his own people and blatantly flouting election rules in 2009 to continue to be in power. *The New York Times* (April 8, 2010) reported that instead of disciplining him the Obama administration humoured him because he had declared in 2009 that he would close the American air base on the outskirts of Bishkek, the country's capital. He changed his mind after the Americans agreed to several concessions and offered a higher rent for the base. In other words, because the air base in Kyrgyzstan was of critical importance in the American War in Afghanistan, Kurmanbek Bakiev could get what he wanted from the powerful Americans.

Poverty-stricken Ethiopia (population 77 million) gets US$1 billion in aid from the US every year. Its prime minister, Meles Zenawi, has also been accused by human-rights groups of a repressive regime that includes muzzling of the press. *The Economist* (March 25, 2010) reports that the US goes along quietly because 'the Pentagon needs Ethiopia and its bare-knuckle intelligence service to help keep Al-Qaeda fighters in neighbouring Somalia at bay.' Of course, American officials justify the support for Zenawi saying that he has the best chance of keeping the country together. As in the case of Kyrgyzstan's president, Zenawi is able to get the Americans to put away their sermons on democracy because although poor and in need of a dole out, he can play a strategic role in the American scheme of things.

Being part of the network is like being part of a religious, cultural, political, or linguistic group that gives you a certain shared identity and an obligation to support one another. Everyone can recall instances of receiving special consideration from a stranger just because it emerges during the conversation that there is a common friend.

Networking is not the same as slapping together a consortium for a specific objective. It is an approach to life in which you connect with a range of people and offer them what you have. The help you provide may be a piece of information, introduction to another individual, enthusiastic support for an idea, or a pair of empathic ears. Each time you help someone in the network, you build up a deposit and enhance your 'ethos' and power to persuade.

You may be able to use social networking sites to influence your peers. You may be part of different networks that intersect. That itself makes you an influential member of the network because, for several of your peers and bosses, you may be the gateway to another network.

If you say good things about your peers in public, you create in them a subtle debt of gratitude towards you. This should not be adoption of a mere technique or tactic but development of a generally generous approach towards your peers. When we judge others, we raise the bar so much that most of them can't touch it, let alone jump over. We find little to admire and plenty to sneer at. This has to change. We need to learn to judge others by the same yardstick as we judge ourselves by and give credit to others for their contributions. Adoption of this approach creates goodwill and cements the mutual dependence that is useful in peer-persuasion attempts.

Peers in an organization are technically equal among themselves just as citizens in a country are all equal in the eyes of the law. But in reality, some are 'more equal.' They enjoy far more social power than the others because of factors such as age, expertise, and proximity to people in power. Gender also can be a factor because males tend to have more power than females in comparable positions. Monica Gaughan of Georgia Institute of Technology, for example, found that while there was mutual influence among adolescents in 'same-sex best friendships,' the influence over drinking patterns was one-way in 'mixed-sex best friendships': boys influenced their female friends' drinking patterns, not the other way round. Thus, mutual dependence is loaded in favour of some. That definitely enhances their persuasiveness because it gives them coercive and reward power over their peers to some extent. That power to give social rewards and punishments comes to them not from the organizational position they hold but from the network they cultivate. The peers who get persuaded by them may give noble reasons for their compliance, but the real story will be one of carrot and stick.

CONCLUSION

Most successful managers are good at leading their peers and getting their support for their initiatives. They achieve this through persuasion rather than manipulation. Persuading peers is tough, but it is worth honing that skill because it raises your stock and enhances your ability to persuade your bosses as well as subordinates.

LESSONS LEARNT

- Peer persuasion tends to take long; patience is essential for success.
- Ridiculing those who hold out can be counter-productive.
- Personal example is a powerful factor in persuading your peers to accept your ideas.
- For persuading peers several techniques are available: ego-stroking, getting crowd support, bargaining and offering exchanges, making personal appeals, quoting rules and traditions, consulting and seeking advice, and logical reasoning.
- Generally, a combination of two or more techniques of persuasion may be required.
- When persuading peers in groups, practice the strategy of persuasion cascade to ensure success.
- For your persuasion efforts to succeed you need to take a strategic, long-term approach to becoming persuasive.
- Your long-term strategy should include developing a reputation for expertise in some field, increasing your visibility, and networking.

We have so far looked at persuasion within the organization. It is time now to go beyond the organization and to examine the best ways of persuading customers whose wholehearted support your company needs in order to thrive.

REFERENCES

Caillaud, B. and J. Tirole (2007). 'Consensus Building: How to Persuade a Group'. *The American Economic Review*, 97(5), pp. 1877–1900.

Gaughan, M. (2006). 'The Gender Structure of Adolescent Peer Influence on Drinking'. *Journal of Health and Social Behavior*, 47 (March), pp. 47–61.

Griskevicius, V., R. B. Cialdini, and N. J. Goldstein (2008). 'Applying (and Resisting) Peer Influence'. *MIT Sloan Management Review*. 49(2), pp. 84–8.

Hall, K.W. (2010). 'Using Peer Pressure to Improve Performance'. *Harvard Business Review South Asia*, (April 2010), p. 47.

Keys, B. and T. Case (1990). 'How to Become an Influential Manager'. *The Executive*, 4(4), pp. 38–51.

Shenkar, O. (2010). *Copycats: How Smart Companies Use Imitation to Gain a Strategic Edge*. Boston: Harvard Business Press.

6

The Persuasive Vendor

INTRODUCTION

Whatever your designation in your organization, you will need to wear the vendor's hat from time to time and sell products or services to external or internal customers, or both. In this chapter we shall explore how to be a persuasive vendor. What distinguishes the vendor–customer relationship from other relationships involving persuasion is that here the persuadee generally has the upper hand.

A vendor's main strength is that he is selling a product or service for which there is demand. His main weakness is that there is competition from others who may have more attractive offers. Faced with existing or anticipated competition, vendors who have some monopolistic clout try to lock the customers in by making it difficult or expensive for them to switch to a rival's product or service. Another move many vendors make is to rely on lies and half-truths to attract or retain customers. Although both these are temptations to which a large number of companies including multinationals yield, you must resist both if you want to be a persuasive vendor.

If you adopt a short-sighted approach to selling, each sale may bring in a tidy profit but the customer may never come back because she may not trust you again. The trouble with this approach is that the business cannot grow big. If you adopt the high-street shopkeeper's approach, your credibility and trustworthiness will attract new customers while retaining old ones who will be your ambassadors.

Your customers are individuals even when your contract is with companies. As a result, being liked, trusted, and respected as a person is important for you to be able to persuade your potential customers. Those who lie and mislead their customers are unlikely to build the credibility required for sustained persuasiveness and long-term success.

While a pleasant personality and credibility dispose potential customers favourably towards you, you need to understand their requirements, limitations, and priorities in order to frame your product or service appropriately. It is hard to find products that you can sell on the basis of their uniqueness; the edge has to come from service that exceeds customer expectations. No one can copy service that is truly tailor-made for customers. Against the background of such long-term strategies, you can employ specific persuasive techniques to become more persuasive and facilitate sales for your organization.

YOUR STRENGTHS AND WEAKNESSES AS A VENDOR

If you are a vendor, you sell products or services. Your main strength is that there is demand for what you offer. You meet a need; hence you are in business. It is the quality of demand that raises or lowers the perceived value of what you offer, not just the changing equation between supply and demand. In May 2010, for example, someone paid US$106.5 million for 'Nude, Green Leaves and Bust,' a 1932 Pablo Picasso painting. The supply, one painting, has remained the same all these years; it is the demand and, consequently, the perceived value that have been going up and pushing the price up.

People are always looking for goods and services that will help them live and work better. They are willing to exchange their cash, their possessions, or certain services for goods and services that they are looking for. But then, this is also your main weakness as a vendor. If they don't perceive that your offering gives them what they are looking for, they will not be interested even if you are convinced that you are the one they should be buying from. Or, if they find that someone else's offering fits their needs better or gives them better value, they move over. Thus, investors, who gladly paid US$50 apiece for Citibank shares in March 2007, were reluctant to pay even one dollar for the same shares two years later. Mahatma Gandhi describes it very well: '[The customer] is not dependent on us. We are dependent on him... We are not doing him a favour by serving him. He is doing us a favour by giving us an opportunity to do so.'

A vendor is like a plant in a garden. It grows and produces flowers and fruits. The gardener allows it to grow if he believes that it will be useful in some respect. It may be the plant's roots, stem, leaves, flowers, or fruits that he finds useful. It may be the plant's medicinal properties or edibility, or pleasing appearance that he values. If the plant doesn't meet any of his needs, it is treated as a weed and destroyed. It is possible that the plant has some magical powers, but as long as the gardener is unaware of them, it is no better than a weed. The equation therefore is very clear. *The vendor—customer relationship is one of mutual dependence. It is a partnership, but the customer generally has the upper hand.*

If you want to succeed as a vendor, you need to find or create demand for your goods and services. Unfortunately, you are unlikely to get a free run of the place even if you have products and services for which there is good demand. Although Michael Porter has rightly put the bargaining power of suppliers among the five competitive forces that shape an entire industry, most of the time you will have competition from other suppliers, whatever be the goods or services you offer and whatever the price you demand. Your customers have a choice. There is hardly any successful product or service that will not attract imitators. You have to pull potential customers to your goods and services away from your competitors. The only genuine tool you have for accomplishing this is persuasion. People should buy from you because they are convinced that you meet their requirements better than your competitors. If you don't, you will do well to adapt your product or service to them (see box, Long Pursuit).

LONG PURSUIT

When I joined Voltas as General Manager of Corporate Planning in 2004, the procurement process there was not as streamlined as at one of its sister companies where I had been working previously. This was not surprising. Voltas was a highly diversified engineering projects company and so its procurement process was fragmented across locations and projects. I felt that Voltas could save money by improving procurement practices. Aggregating purchases and strategising for different categories, for example. But when you consider the diversified nature of the business and the organizational dynamics, it was a tall order. I wished there was some way to at least get the different units to see what the others were buying. I knew that e-procurement would provide such visibility across units. It would also help reduce costs because different suppliers would compete among themselves for business. Transparency would be a bonus.

I mentioned it to a former colleague who had joined Krona (name changed), an American multinational and a leading supplier of e-auction platform software. He was excited. He thought that for Krona it would be a simple jump from one Tata company, where its software was being used successfully, to another. He had not anticipated the main hurdle: Krona's expertise was in manufacturing companies; it did not have experience relevant to engineering projects companies like Voltas. But they were very keen on selling to us because we were growing at 40 percent year-on-year and we were present in many countries. If we adopted their software, we would be a 'big catch,' a major reference point for Krona to sell it to many more companies managing projects.

There was one more hurdle. Although I was convinced about the value of the e-auction platform, I was not at all sure that all SBUs would welcome it. Each unit had autonomy in procurement and had its own procedure. This uncertainty led to yet another problem. Krona's model of doing business—signing contracts linked to the number of user licenses—where the initial fixed costs are very high. We would obviously not want to incur very high fixed costs when we were not at all sure how many units would adopt the platform. There was no way one SBU could force it on other units.

In about eighteen months, Krona came up with a few cases of small project management companies using its software successfully. But the problem with the billing model continued. Now I was keen on buying the software; I was equally certain that Krona should change the billing model for us so that our initial fixed costs would be low.

I told Krona that we could save the deal only if they changed their standard billing model. We wanted them to start with low fixed costs. I promised to share with them a part of the procurement savings that we make through the adoption of the software. It would gradually become profitable for them as more units adopted the software.

They would also get additional business from other project management companies that can be given Voltas's reference. Finally, Krona agreed to change its billing model to suit our peculiar circumstances.

Source: As narrated by Prasanna Pahade, General Manager, Corporate Planning, Voltas Limited.

THE VENDOR'S TEMPTATIONS

Pulling customers away from competition through genuine persuasion is hard work, especially when you don't have a distinctly superior product or service to offer. The right approach should then be to work towards making the product or service superior. But that is even harder. So many vendors are buffeted by at least one of two temptations: shackle customers or mislead them. Sadly, a large number of vendors yield to either of these temptations without putting up a fight.

Locking Customers In

During the 1970s and 80s, many domestic cooking gas distribution agencies in India would not release a new connection allotted to you after a long wait unless you bought a stove from them at an inflated price. Many retailers in the state Public Distribution System force customers even now to buy certain damaged or slow-moving items if they want to buy other items in great demand. Such forced bundling doesn't give the customer any benefit; rather, it is an abuse of the monopolistic power those small-time vendors enjoy in their tiny kingdoms.

Whenever commercial organizations enjoy monopolistic power, either because they have government backing or because they have a dominant market share, they use coercion rather than persuasion to prevent customers from going to competitors. Let's take the case of Air India. Several passengers you see on board this public sector carrier's flights are there because those flights fit their schedule and purse better than competitors' flights; some passengers, however, are there not because they want to be but because they have no choice. They are government employees flying on work or taking leave travel concession; the government would reimburse their airfares only if they flew Air India. The company got the government to introduce this condition when it found passengers courting other more efficient and customer-friendly airlines.

Many well known global software companies including IBM, Microsoft, and Apple use their dominant market position to lock their customers in and generate easy profits without competing fairly with other vendors. So do many big telecom companies. They all virtually imprison their customers by making it difficult or expensive for them to switch to alternative vendors and obtain better service. These multinational giants are no better in this respect than the small-town cooking-gas agency or the village retailer in the Public Distribution System. The multinationals are simply better at masking such coercion and presenting it as protection of standards and intellectual property rights.

That many global companies indulge in such unfair practices is not a good enough reason for us to adopt them when we smell some monopolistic power vis-à-vis our customers. We may be able to generate short-term profits through such use of clout but when we try to hold a lot of unhappy and unwilling customers to ransom, we should expect a rebellion sooner or later. The trouble with rebellion is that it doesn't make a distinction between right and wrong—like molten lava it may destroy everything that comes in its path.

This kind of entrapment is different from the friendly lock-in frequent shoppers including regular flyers experience. Customers voluntarily join such clubs because the membership gives them special privileges and discounts even as the vendors benefit from customer retention. There may also be bundling of goods and services in which the vendor passes on to the customer part of the savings. The main difference is that such a marriage is not forced upon the customer.

Misleading Customers

Not many vendors hold monopolistic power over their customers. The temptation to use force, therefore, is neither strong nor common. The more widespread temptation is to mislead customers into buying products and services by making false claims or by hiding critical information that might make them hesitant. Many vendors look at the customer as someone to outwit rather than serve. Their endeavour is to separate her from her money by hook or by crook. They believe that all is fair in business. They consider clever, legally safe lying as one of the principal ploys in the vendor's repertoire.

It is natural that vendors highlight the positives and the benefits of their product or service when they try to sell it. It is up to the customer to ask them questions about aspects of the product or service that worry her. This is because different customers may have different priorities. But vendors should not lie to sell their product or service because they and their customers are mutually dependent partners. Maintaining trust is critical for both if they are interested in a long-term relationship. In general, the vendor stands to gain more from a long-term relationship.

Lying occurs in two ways. First, a vendor states something that he knows to be untrue. If, for example, he claims that his product has been certified by the Bureau of Indian Standards (BIS) when it has not been, he is lying to make a sale. Second, the vendor withholds information which he is legally bound to disclose. If, for example, a pharmaceutical company suppresses information about the adverse effects of a drug in order to get regulatory approval, it is lying (see box, Lying, Pharma-style). Sadly, it is not at all uncommon.

LYING, PHARMA-STYLE

According to an editorial in *The Hindu* (September 1, 2009), the American pharmaceutical company Wyeth hired professional ghostwriters to publish papers in medical journals. Those papers presented Wyeth's popular hormone therapy drug Prempro, generally prescribed to menopausal women, as very good. They did not make any reference to the growing evidence of higher breast cancer risk for those who take the drug.

An editorial in the *New York Times* (July 14, 2010) commented on the way GlaxoSmithKline hid the heart risks associated with its diabetes drug Avandia, and stated that GlaxoSmithKline 'can't be trusted to report adverse clinical results fairly.'

Often junior and middle-level managers do not realize they are lying to their customers when they make certain claims confidently. The simple reason is that they are passing on, without any hesitation whatsoever, information which they consider to be true. The lying has taken place at a different level internally. The senior management has lied to them either by making false claims or by suppressing unflattering information. The managers at lower levels merely toe the company line because they have no reason to believe that their seniors have given them false information. They are rather like an innocent international passenger who carries a banned drug assuming that the little parcel that an acquaintance handed her at the airport was a special birthday gift, which would be picked up by a friend's friend at the destination. She signs all kinds of declarations and walks confidently through the Customs unperturbed because she is unaware of the contraband she is carrying.

As we have seen in Chapter 2, credibility is the engine that drives persuasion. Once your credibility is lost, others may not accept even the truth that you tell. Credibility, therefore, is a treasure that you should guard with all your might if you want to be a persuasive vendor rather than a product-pusher.

THE RAILWAY-PLATFORM APPROACH TO SELLING

Your train stops at a busy station for five minutes. You spot on the platform a man selling fresh oranges, apparently from the nearby farms. You ask him if the oranges are sweet. He says they are and offers to give you a sample segment from a peeled orange in his hand. You don't taste it but his confidence reassures you. He quotes Rs 60 for a dozen. You bargain a little and bring the price down to Rs 50. You pay him and take the bag from his hands as the train starts moving. You are ecstatic about this little triumph because in your city you have to pay at least Rs 90 for it.

When you open the bag back at home, however, you discover that there are just ten oranges out of which only the three ones at the top are sweet. The rest are not fresh either. You feel angry with yourself and with the hawker. He did not force it on you.

Rather, he persuaded you effortlessly to part with your money for that junk. The sight of orchards as the train approached the station, the smell of a great bargain, and the extreme shortage of time for checking and decision-making led to such a silly purchase. You will never want to buy anything from that vendor ever again. Perhaps you will resolve never to buy anything from railway-platform hawkers.

The orange seller has lost a customer forever. He doesn't care. The next train will bring more suckers. His business model doesn't depend on repeat customers. He knows he has to find a new customer for each sale, but he makes a fat profit on each sale.

Vendors have a choice between this hawker's sales strategy and the High Street shopkeeper's sales strategy. If you adopt the hawker's strategy, you may be able to palm inferior products or services off to uncritical customers and enjoy a high profit margin. The trouble is that by stopping customers from coming back to you or from recommending you to their friends and acquaintances, you are stopping your business from growing. Year after year the orange seller walks along moving trains at the same railway station, selling bags of oranges. The scale of his business does not grow. Most of a High Street shopkeeper's sales come from a growing circle of happy, repeat customers, their friends, and relations. They help his business grow.

You may be able to scale up your business by fooling a lot of people without your credibility getting dented. But someday, when you least expect it, the bubble may burst as 'Big Bull' stockbroker Harshad Mehta in India and Bernard Madoff of Bernard L. Madoff Investment Securities in the US, among many others, discovered. The higher you go the harder you fall.

VENDORS' LONG-TERM STRATEGIES

> Your long-term strategy should be to build up a warm and pleasant personality along with a reputation as someone who is fair, someone who delivers value to the customer, someone who will not exploit her weaknesses, someone who can be trusted.

A fundamental principle vendors should keep in mind is that customers are always individuals or groups of individuals, never organizations. They may be buying products and services either for themselves or for their organizations. Any legal contract may be between two organizations, but the transactions are between individuals, not between abstract entities. If we ignore this important factor when we attempt to persuade our potential customers to buy our products or services, we will be heading towards trouble.

One of the immediate implications is that ethos and pathos—persuader's personality and persuadee's emotions—play an important role in purchase decisions. Simply restated, the persuasive power of your attempt to sell a product or service is likely to be enhanced significantly if the potential customer likes you, trusts you, and respects you. It is common experience that we don't mind forgoing some benefits we are entitled to in order to please someone we like. In some negotiations a minor factor like that may stand between your sealing a deal, and seeing your customer walk away.

If you want to be a persuasive vendor and get a definite edge over your competitors who offer similar products or services, your long-term strategy should be to build up a warm and pleasant personality along with a reputation as a fair and trustworthy vendor. Individuals, who deal with you either for themselves or on behalf of their organizations, should trust you and feel comfortable dealing with you to go ahead and buy from you, especially when major purchase decisions are involved (see box, Game Changer).

GAME CHANGER

In the third quarter of 1982, Suzuki Motor Company (SMC) of Japan and the Indian government were getting ready to finalize a joint-venture agreement to produce passenger cars in India under the brand name Maruti. The Indian side wanted SMC to take 40 percent of the equity in Maruti Udyog Ltd. For various reasons SMC was unwilling to buy more than 25 percent (amounting to US$22 million). And they made that position very clear. Then R.C. Bhargava of the Indian side explained to SMC that they would get additional statutory benefits under the Indian Companies Act if, as a minority shareholder, they held 26 percent equity. SMC immediately agreed to raise their equity share from 25 to 26 percent.

Bhargava recalls that the benefit Maruti received for this simple act of explaining the benefit of taking an additional 1 percent equity was gain in SMC's trust. Operationally this would not make any difference in the joint-venture. But his pointing out the additional legal rights SMC would get 'helped in building the feeling that we would work in a fair and transparent manner' (p. 48). In the initial stages of a joint venture between a foreign private company and Indian government, the enormous value of such trust is self evident.

Source: R.C. Bhargava, *The Maruti Story: How a Public Sector Company Put India on Wheels*, 2010. Noida: Collins Business, p. 48.

Ultimately, all this boils down to your credibility. That is why lying is not an option if you want to be a persuasive vendor. You may be able to make a profitable sale or two by lying to and misleading your customer, but you will not be able to sustain the railway-platform hawker's model for long if you want to grow. If you rise, in spite of it, a miserable fall is just a matter of time.

Of course, a pleasant personality and the reputation for trustworthiness alone cannot clinch a deal, especially if the customer represents an organization. She will have to justify her purchase decisions to her organization with the help of hard data. Your pleasant behaviour and credibility will present the hard data in the most appealing fashion. That is all. But that is a lot when you are competing with others who offer products or services similar to yours.

In *Getting to Yes: Negotiating Agreement without Giving* in, Roger Fisher and William Ury give three norms to judge negotiations.

- ▶ The agreement reached should be wise. (A wise agreement meets the legitimate interests of both sides.)
- ▶ It should be efficient.
- ▶ It should improve or at least maintain the relationship between the two parties.

These capture the relationship between vendors and customers because all selling is, in a sense, exchange. You exchange your product or service for money or for some other product or service. When you perform this exchange in such a way that both you and your customer are happy with the outcome, you win a customer over rather than merely make a sale. If she perceives that she has had a raw deal from you or that she has been tricked into a bad purchase, you win the battle but lose the war. This is especially true of major purchases with long-term consequences.

The product or service you sell may be fantastic. But your customers will take interest in it, learn more about it, and buy it only if they perceive it as something they are looking for consciously or unconsciously. The secret behind the creation of such a perception is appropriate framing or positioning by the vendor. You will not, however, be able to choose the right frame if you don't understand them, their needs, their values, their attitudes, their hopes, their concerns, their goals, their priorities, their limitations, and so on. Are they, for instance, looking to reduce their costs? Enhance their profits? Increase their market share? Improve their customer service? Brighten their image? Perhaps your product or service will do all this, especially cost reduction. But the right framing will be to project its ability to increase their market share if you figure out that that is their priority. Perhaps cost reduction does not excite them as much as a quick rise in market share.

Here is a story, most probably apocryphal, narrated by Kurt Mortensen in Magnetic Persuasion (www.magneticpersuasion. com), which illustrates in a humorous way how framing works. The story is about Airman Jones at the US Army's GI induction centre. It was his job to encourage GIs to take out insurance. Captain Smith noticed that Jones had been phenomenally successful. Intrigued, he sneaked into the hall during one of Jones's presentations to find out the secret of his success. And this is what Captain Smith heard Jones say: 'Did you know that if you have GI insurance and you're killed in action, the government has to pay at least US$200,000 to your beneficiaries? But if you're killed in action without GI insurance, the government has to pay only US$6,000! Now, any guesses who they'll send into battle FIRST?'

The key to effective framing, then, is a thorough understanding of the potential customer. But many customers will not tell you up front what they are looking for. They may not even know what they really need. Apart from asking intelligent questions, you need to invest time and effort to understand them by studying their actions.

In 'The Chinese Culinary Invasion', author Vikram Doctor attributes the popularity of Chinese restaurants all over the world to their ability to adapt their cuisine to meet the diverse expectations of customers in different regions, cultures, and sub cultures. They have products that fit pockets of all sizes. Their process of adapting themselves to diverse needs is so successful that 'Indians who are averse to food of other Indian communities, will happily come together around a Chinese restaurant table.'

Many companies that do business on the Internet quietly gather information about their customers by monitoring their online actions. What sites do they visit most frequently? What kind of things do they buy online? What kind of advertisements do they click on? How long do they spend at each stop? And so on. This helps Internet companies expose you to what is most likely to interest you and what you are most likely to buy. If you search for *The Essentials of Negotiation* on Amazon.com, for example, you will be presented with information on that book as well as on other popular books dealing with negotiation. Amazon.com will not show you fascinating books on the origins of Western classical music or the rise of Taliban.

If it is business to business selling, you will need to understand your customer's customers also, as Ram Charan says in *What the Customer Wants You to Know*. If you are a manufacturer of chemicals, for example, you supply certain formulations to a company that makes and supplies insecticides or detergents to a retail chain from which the ultimate customer buys them. It is in your interest to keep in mind the concerns not only of your immediate customer but also of the retailer and of the ultimate consumers because if they go away, your direct customer will abandon you sooner or later. Charan says that knowledge about your customer's customers will help you position your product or service almost seductively to your customer.

There is an additional challenge in business to business transactions. There may be several managers with different perspectives weighing in on a purchase decision. This makes framing your product or service harder but all the more important. Ram Charan explains it with the example of a consumer-goods company that buys packaging. The purchasing manager may be interested in low price, good quality, and reliable delivery. The marketing manager may be more interested in how the packaging affects shelf space at the retailers and the product's brand image. The public-relations manager's main concern may be whether the packaging is environment friendly. If a vendor can present her package as recyclable, consistent with the customer's brand image, economical, and efficient in shelf space usage, says Ram Charan, the product will appeal to many in the customer's organization.

There are times when you may not be able to find an angle from which they can perceive your product or service as adding value. You may then have to modify your product or service to meet their needs and limitations. That is what Pauline Lewis, founder of the handbag company Oovoo Designs in Alexandria, Virginia, did in 2008. She found that because of recession her customers were reluctant to buy her purses and bags priced from US$99 although they loved the brand. She did not want to slash the price and dilute the brand. So she introduced a new product, a cellphone holder, with the embroidery that had made her handbag popular. Her customers welcomed it warmly, says Jeremy Quittner in *How to Boost Sales by Down-Selling Your Customers*.

It is increasingly difficult to claim a unique feature for any product or service. If there is any special feature, there will soon be imitations superior to the originals. Where you really add value is the way you deliver the service. In *Moments of Magic*, Tony Alessandra says, 'Being on par in terms of price and quality only gets you into the game. Service wins the game.' While he was referring to product versus service, his distinction is applicable to service versus service also. The same 'service' can be delivered differently. The persuasive vendor's aim should be to win the customer over and retain her through service that goes beyond her expectations. Selling will take care of itself.

Frank Farrell of Ottawa, Canada, narrates the following incident in, *Anyone may copy this service from Xerox*. On a Friday, the display panel of the colour laser printer (XEROX 8550) in his office stopped working. The authorized dealer he contacted quoted US$240 (part: US$140; service: US$100) for fixing it. Before asking the dealer to send an engineer, he called Xerox Service. The woman who answered the phone diagnosed the problem immediately, and even figured out the error number displayed by the printer. Although it was well past the warranty period, she offered to send a replacement part free. On Monday, Frank was delighted to receive the part along with instructions on how to install it. He was so touched that he wrote about this incident and added, ecstatically: 'I would recommend Xerox to anyone. Their products are great and their service is amazing. You get a real sense that Xerox employees really enjoy working there and that translates into great service.'

By going well beyond Frank's expectations, the Xerox employee became a persuasive vendor to him. She would now be able to sell him any Xerox product or service contract with little or no effort. In Frank's eyes, she was Xerox, and Xerox was the epitome of service that delighted customers. He would now be an ideal, lifelong Xerox fan because he would spread details of the good experience far and wide not only by talking about it but also by writing about it.

It is very instructive to study one of the reader responses to Frank's post. On September 2, 2009, a reader called Reginald wrote that Xerox's response was 'not a great service, just fixing a defect.' He went on to state that defective panels were 'a known problem with XEROX 8500/8550.' That is why the Xerox employee who answered the phone readily figured out the error number and replaced the panel free. Of course, the dealer who said he would charge US$240 was going to take advantage of Frank's ignorance.

If Reginald's explanation is true, it may dilute Frank's delight a little, but not take it away. After all, he had used the printer for three years without the panel giving him any trouble. When a problem cropped up, the Xerox employee acted promptly and solved his problem over the weekend without charging him anything. This should delight anyone in Frank's position. Without the information that Xerox would replace that part free of charge *for anyone* who had bought that machine, Frank's delight would be boundless. It is rarely that someone in Frank's position has full information about what the company would replace free. Generally, the terms of contract are worded heavily in favour of the vendor. Frank's enthusiastic response illustrates one of Peter Drucker's sayings: 'Quality in a service or product is not what you put into it. It is what the client or customer gets out of it.'

Should the Xerox employee have told Frank that the replacement was free because the company had found manufacturing defects in some of those panels? Certainly not. Unless, of course, she was specifically asked. Here, the Xerox employee's framing was excellent. She diagnosed the problem correctly from the description Frank gave her, and promptly sent him the part without charging him anything although he had told her that the machine was well past the warranty period. That delighted Frank who was worried about possible dent to productivity in his office for several days. If the Xerox employee had said that she was surprised because she had not come across any problem with the panel so far, but would send a replacement part free, she would be telling a lie to enhance the customer's delight. That, however, would be unacceptable and undesirable. Any such lie would carry a significant risk of loss of trust and credibility.

VENDORS' SHORT-TERM STRATEGIES

While a pleasant personality and high credibility may open many customer doors, you need other persuasive moves to sell successfully especially if the resistance is high. Let's listen to the first person account of a CEO on how his boss sold him an idea that he had resisted repeatedly:

I am the CEO of Ready Made Garments (RMG) Division of Bharat Silks Group, Bangalore. I never thought I would be a CEO. In fact, I was pretty sure I shouldn't be. It's not that I'm not ambitious. But a chartered accountant by profession and somewhat shy by nature, I knew I wanted to deal with numbers, not people. And I was doing very well as the company's finance manager in the corporate office. That is when, in 2004, Shyam Sunder Goenka, the company's owner and managing director suggested that I take over RMG, a sick unit of the company.

I vigorously rejected his suggestion. It was a large unit with 650 to 700 employees. In spite of being managed by an experienced CEO, it was losing money. Being a North Indian, I wouldn't be able to cope with Kannada, the local language. I didn't know anything about the cloth-manufacturing process either. So there was no way this shy chartered accountant would make a sick bird fly. I was surprised that a shrewd businessman like Mr Goenka should make such a preposterous suggestion. But I did become its CEO, turned it around, and now it accounts for 45 percent of the group's turnover. Let me tell you the story.

Mr Goenka didn't give up when he got a quick and firm no from me. He said that he saw an entrepreneur in me. Me? An entrepreneur? I wasn't so naïve as to swallow such bull. I laughed it away. But he persisted. 'I did an experiment,' he said. 'And it proved my hunch.' I was curious. What hunch? What experiment? He continued: 'Recently I asked you to step in and help the Home Furnishings unit when its CEO went away on a month's leave. Instead of warming the chair, you studied the way trade enquiries were being handled. You realized that junior staff was doing it without any support from the seniors. You involved yourself and, as a result, you landed a big order.'

'Ah, yes, but it was a small, well-run unit with just about 60 workers,' I cut in because I wanted to tell him that I was merely swimming downstream. 'Maybe, but what matters is the way you took charge,' he added. 'It clearly shows your potential.'

I was still far from convinced. Mr Goenka changed the track. 'Okay, don't take charge,' he said. 'Just go over to RMG from time to time and help the CEO get more orders.' This I accepted.

In a few weeks the RMG CEO resigned. Now that I was familiar with the garments unit, Mr Goenka urged me to take over. I was worried I would get stuck there. So I refused again and asked him to look for a proper replacement. He readily agreed, but asked me if I could, in the meanwhile, step in and take charge so that the unit didn't suffer. Of course I agreed.

As with the Home Furnishings unit, I decided to do something rather than just 'look after' the unit. I was amazed at the way things moved. I must say I was pretty successful in getting good orders. Three months later, Mr Goenka still hadn't found a replacement. One day he asked me to hire a deputy to take care of finance in the corporate office so that I could focus on RMG. When he found me still hesitant, he said, 'Give yourself three to four months. If you find the assignment tough, I promise to send you back to the corporate office.'

It is now five years. I thoroughly enjoy being the CEO. And, as I said, we now contribute 45 percent of the group's turnover. (As narrated by Deepak Mittal, CEO, RMG, Bharat Silks, Bangalore).

This is not the usual selling of a product or service. Here, an idea is sold to an extremely reluctant internal customer. It illustrates several micro-strategies used by the seller. It also reassures us that proper persuasion can be a long drawn-out affair and that an initial no, however emphatic, need not stop us. We need to figure out the source of resistance (which the prospect himself may not be aware of), estimate the strength of resistance, and choose the right way to frame our proposal. We may need to try various techniques rather than give up at the first sign of strong resistance if we really believe in our mission.

Goenka makes several moves to sell Mittal the idea that he can be a very successful CEO of a large plant. Before that, he does his homework very well and equips himself with different kinds of persuasion tools because he doesn't know what will work best with Mittal. Goenka strokes his ego by suggesting that he take over as CEO of the RMG unit. Mittal is flattered, as anyone in his position would be, because he respects and admires Goenka as a 'shrewd businessman.' Invitation to be the CEO is praise and approval bundled together. But praise doesn't work on Mittal the way it is supposed to. In fact, it frightens him. That is when Goenka says that he sees an entrepreneur in him. Even that does not work. So Goenka gives him proof drawn from one of his experiments: Mittal has already done a fine job as a stand-in CEO of a smaller unit. All this dilutes the resistance. But his fear of managerial failure based on his deep-seated convictions about his introvert personality is so strong that even that proof is not powerful enough to remove his resistance completely.

Not once does Goenka hassle Mittal. He is persistent but never overbearing. He doesn't tell lies. He gets small commitments from Mittal. Each time he explains away his success, Goenka helps him enhance his self-perception and confirms Goenka's assessment of him as an entrepreneur capable of running an industrial unit successfully. Although Mittal's self-image is that of an introvert, incapable of managing people, Goenka rightly infers from his behaviour that he is capable and ambitious but held back by certain fears. That is why he helps Mittal change his self-perception with a series of increasingly stronger proofs.

CONCLUSION

Managers have to wear the vendor's hat and persuade both internal and external customers to buy their products, services, and ideas. In order to do so persuasively, they have to hone long-term as well as short-term strategies. Fundamental to a persuasive personality is credibility. Equally important is warmth towards potential customers. But they will merely open the customer's door. Appropriate framing of the product or service based on a deep understanding of the customer's needs, limitations, and priorities is essential for the sale to take place. This is where mastering short-term persuasive strategies comes in handy.

LESSONS LEARNT

▶ The vendor-customer relationship is one of mutually dependent partnership, but the customer tends to have the upper hand.

▶ A vendor's strength is that there is demand for his products or services; his weakness is that there is competition that could drive his customers away.

▶ The two major temptations that buffet vendors are to use monopolistic power to hold the customer back against his wishes and to mislead him through lies and half-truths.

▶ You may be able to make short term profits by following the railway-platform hawker's approach to selling, but you cannot sustain it in the long term if you want to grow your business.

▶ A warm and pleasant personality is extremely important in a vendor because buying and selling are by individuals even when the contracts are between organizations.

▶ Personal factors, including credibility and trustworthiness, will only open the customer's door. You will need hard data and rational evidence to clinch the deal especially in organizational selling.

A persuader may use the spoken medium or the written medium to reach out to her target. Each medium has its own advantages and disadvantages. We need to be aware of them for us to choose the right medium and use it efficiently. So we shall now turn to the spoken medium.

REFERENCES

Alessandra, T. (2003). *Moments of Magic*. http://www.expertmagazine. com/EMOnline/RC/magic.htm (last accessed on 10 May, 2010).

Bhargava, R. C. (2010). *The Maruti Story: How a Public Sector Company Put India on Wheels*. Noida: Collins Business

Charan, R. (2007). *What the Customer Wants You to Know: How Everybody Needs to Think Differently about Sales*. New Delhi: Penguin.

Doctor V. (June 1, 2010). 'The Chinese Culinary Invasion: The Great Selling Point of Chinese restaurants is the Way They Adapt to Meet Expectations'. *The Economic Times* (Ahmedabad edition), p. 12.

Farrell, F. (n. d.) 'Anyone may copy this service from Xerox'. Accessed on July 22, 2010 from http://www.customerservicepoint.com/anyone-may-copy-this-service-from-xerox.html

Fisher, R. and W. Ury (1987). *Getting To Yes: Negotiating Agreement Without Giving In*. London: Arrow Books.

Porter, M.E. (2008). The Five Competitive Forces That Shape Strategy. *Harvard Business Review*. http://hbr.org/2008/01/the-five-competitive-forces-that-shape-strategy/ar/1

Quittner, J. (2010). *How to Boost Sales by Down-Selling Your Customers*. http://www.bnet.com/2403-13241_23-399338.html (last accessed on May 14, 2010).

7

The Persuasive Speaker

INTRODUCTION

So far we have looked at different aspects of persuasion without focusing on the medium, spoken or written. It is time to examine the role played by it, to check which medium is more appropriate under what conditions, and to explore ways of becoming more persuasive when we use one medium or the other. In this chapter we shall focus on oral persuasion.

Whether spoken or written, the basic principles of persuasion are the same. There are, however, differences in the way we work the two mediums and influence our target. The spoken medium is the easier of the two. In order to use it effectively, however, we need to be aware of the factors that enhance oral persuasion.

Ethos and pathos are more important than logos in oral persuasion. You have to enhance your ethos because if your persuadees perceive you as likeable, credible, knowledgeable, fair-minded, and trustworthy, your proposal has a very good chance of being accepted even if your audience does not fully understand it or its implications. The first step is to build up self-belief and self-confidence vis-à-vis your audience. The second step is to grow your reputation.

Persuasion takes place only when the proposal is framed to match the target's needs, priorities, and limitations. Appropriate framing requires strategic planning. To be persuasive, you must follow the top-down approach: show the audience almost at the start the benefits they get from your proposal. Your strategic planning also determines what combination of persuasion techniques you should use.

To persuade an audience you must first build rapport with the members through right words and right non-verbal behaviour. Instead of worrying about your non-verbal behaviour that you cannot control, you should focus on what you can control and refine those aspects. Be authentic. Be passionate about what you propose. These will take care of a lot of problems you face when you speak to persuade.

You must welcome an opportunity to interact with your audience through questions and answers. This is when you will get to know the real resistance to your idea and deal with it. You are also likely to speak with animation when you get into the question-and-answer mode. But you must prepare yourself thoroughly, especially through a rehearsal, to answer questions from the audience.

Technology is a double-edged sword when it comes to oral persuasion. You have to use it wisely to maximize the benefits of technology and minimize its ill effects.

SPEAKERS ARE FROM KOVALAM...

Men are from Mars, Women are from Venus, claimed John Gray very memorably and somewhat simplistically. In a similar vein we can say, 'Speakers are from Kovalam, writers are from Everest.' Kovalam is a warm beach town; anyone can walk in without any difficulty, and many people do. Everest is a remote and freezing cold mountaintop in the Himalayas. Very few people manage to climb it and deal with the loneliness there.

This division is, indeed, a gross simplification because the same person can speak as well as write to persuade. The underlying principles of spoken and written persuasion are the same. Yet, there is some truth in this characterization because the spoken medium is as different from the written medium as a wet and crowded beach is from a lonely, freezing mountaintop. There are major differences in the way the targets are influenced. It is important to recognize those differences if we want to choose the right medium for our persuasive attempts and improve our effectiveness in both these mediums.

The spoken medium is easily accessible to everyone. It requires little training to use it. Infants use it as effectively as adults. Although it is possible to separate speaking and listening in space and time, they generally occur simultaneously. *Appearances* play a far more important role than accurate information processing or reasoning in oral persuasion. It is, therefore, not unusual for those who pack their oral presentations with solid information and indisputable evidence to find their audience uninterested and unmoved. To their chagrin, their rivals with much less substance and more show sell better.

In the next chapter we shall look in greater depth at the process of persuasion through writing. Here, we shall focus on the oral medium. We shall examine the persuasive strategies speakers employ in one-to-one settings, one-to-some settings, and one-to-many settings. We shall, however, pay special attention to persuasive public speaking and presentation because it introduces additional difficulties for persuaders.

THE PERSUASION FACTORS

In Chapter 2, we touched upon the three persuasion factors identified by Aristotle: ethos, pathos, and logos. We also noted that of these three factors, the first two are the most important in your persuasion attempts. This is particularly true of oral persuasion whether you try to persuade one individual or one hundred. Being rational animals, we cannot do without logos. It is used in what we say, that is, in the content of speech. But in oral persuasion it often serves to justify decisions taken under the influence of ethos and pathos; it is rarely the driving force behind decision-making. Clever persuaders employ techniques that lull the target's mind because if he starts questioning the logic of a proposal, it will be difficult to convince him, as we have seen in Chapter 2.

In this section we shall deal with how to enhance your ethos vis-à-vis your audience, most of which has to be done before you open your mouth to speak. We shall deal with pathos in the section on delivery because it is mainly during the delivery of speech that a speaker arouses the audience's emotions.

How to Enhance Your Ethos

We have already seen that your ethos consists of your character and your personality. If your persuadees perceive you as likeable, credible, knowledgeable, fair-minded, and trustworthy, your proposal has a very good chance of being accepted even if they do not fully understand it or its implications. If you display the right kind of ethos, it gently ushers the audience's mind to the seat you have set aside for it. How can you manage it? Obviously, it is not something that you can achieve overnight or develop exclusively for a specific persuasion attempt. It certainly is not a matter of techniques. It should be part of an attempt at being a persuasive person rather than a master of a few persuasive techniques.

Build up self-belief and self-confidence

The very first step is to build up self-belief and self-confidence vis-à-vis your audience. This is important because you will not be able to persuade others if you appear diffident, or you are not sure of yourself, or your products, services, and ideas. Building up self-confidence is also a long-term process. No one goes through life without ever suffering from self-doubt and diffidence. You have to overcome it if you want to be a persuasive speaker (see box, To Sell or Not to Sell).

TO SELL OR NOT TO SELL

'Would you like to sell Infosys for US$1 million?' When N.R. Narayana Murthy and his co-founders of Infosys received this feeler, several of them were relieved. It was 1990. They had spent a frustrating decade growing the company under harsh conditions. They had little money to show. Entrepreneurship was so tightly controlled by government officials that they had little freedom to grow although they were aware of the fantastic scope in Information Technology.

For the seven struggling entrepreneurs, in their forties, US$1 million was a lot of money in 1990. So five of them, including Murthy, met in their office in Bangalore to discuss the idea of selling Infosys.

Most of them wanted to get out with some money in the bank. Murthy didn't want to sell. He told them that they had nothing to lose by hanging on to the company that they had nurtured because they were already at the bottom! They were used to hardship. Their wives had given up any hope of their becoming successful. They were running a marathon. He urged them to push along a little longer.

He said he couldn't leave Infosys. He became emotional as he recalled their journey from a small Mumbai apartment in 1981 and the way they faced many challenges. He said he was sure this was the 'the darkest hour before the dawn.'

Then he said something that startled them. If they were bent upon selling the company, he would buy them all out. Of course, everyone knew that he did not have a cent in his pocket. They were struck by Murthy's confidence in the future of Infosys.

That settled it. They decided to hang on. The rest is history.

Source: Based on an account of the meeting in Vikas Pota, *India Inc.: How India's Top Ten Entrepreneurs are Winning Globally*, 2010. London: Nicholas Brealey, pp. 25–6.

When you set out to persuade someone, what makes you feel diffident is your awareness of your own inadequacies vis-à-vis the persuadee's image or reputation. If, for example, she has a reputation for being an expert or for being hypercritical, or if her position is too far above yours in the organizational hierarchy, you may be so overwhelmed that you are unable to articulate your thoughts well. You may forget your lines and make a mess of the limited time you get to persuade her. You have plenty of company if the very sight of an audience of a dozen or so people makes you diffident even when you know you are more knowledgeable than they are.

There are no easy solutions to this commonly felt problem. There is no simple or single path from diffidence to confidence. You have to find your own way and pace. One approach, which works for many, is to be passionate about what you are proposing. You are so convinced and passionate about your proposal that you may have little time to be overwhelmed by the persuadee's expertise. This is one of the secrets of the success of small children when they try to persuade adults who are far superior to them in knowledge, experience, and power. Being passionate also makes you more persuasive when you speak as we shall see in the section on delivering the speech.

Contributing well thought-out ideas, in response to others' presentations at internal meetings, is a gradual and reliable way to strengthen your self-confidence and ability to articulate your views comfortably. It will also help you build up a desirable profile and spread your reputation within your organization. A familiar face, associated with good ideas and great public behaviour, is trusted far more easily than an unfamiliar face. Being seen championing certain causes may also enhance your profile.

Build a Reputation for Trustworthiness and Reliability

An important step towards enhancing your ethos is building a reputation for trustworthiness and commitment to keeping promises. This, again, is a long-term process. It grows through the way you deal with everyone you interact with. A single betrayal of trust can destroy a reputation built over a lifetime. External circumstances beyond your control, such as cancellation of a flight at the last moment, may make it impossible for you to keep certain promises. Others may understand and accept it. Under such circumstances, a failure may not dent your reputation for reliability. But trustworthiness is entirely different. Once you fail the test, many may not give you a second chance.

The discussion so far assumes that your audience knows you. There are many situations where you have to persuade an audience whose members do not know you. What should you do to enhance your ethos in such a situation?

Get Yourself Introduced

If someone your audience respects can introduce you, your ethos will get a tremendous boost. It is a good idea for you to write the text of the introduction and give it to the introducer in advance.

It makes his job easier and ensures that the aspects you want to highlight get appropriate mention. Of course, you should keep the introduction very brief for it to be used at all. If you provide the introducer with an autobiographical extravaganza, chances are it will not be used at all.

Drop A Few Names

You may not always have the luxury of someone introducing you, especially in informal contexts. Then you have to introduce yourself. If you belong to an organization that has a great reputation, mentioning it helps you get a pedestal to stand on and be seen favourably by your audience. Members of your audience will behave like a shopper picking up a product which she has not heard of but she knows is made or marketed by a company with a great reputation for quality and reliability. Subtle name-dropping can also boost your image when you are an unknown speaker. The trick lies in finding out what name will open which door and choosing the appropriate name. Citing names you have no right to use can of course backfire and destroy any credibility you may have had. Similarly, dropping too many names with an obvious intent to impress your audience can also produce just the opposite result.

Strengthen your pathos and logos if ethos is low

If your ethos is low, you have to make up for it by working on pathos and logos, that is, by being passionate and by supplying high-quality data (see box, The Million-Rupee Note). As we have seen in Chapter 4, managers tend to invest heavily in logos when they have to persuade their bosses. It works if the audience is receptive or at least neutral.

THE MILLION-RUPEE NOTE

Pralhad Chhabria, 14, got the biggest shock of his life when he reached into his pyjama pockets. The 10-rupee note which he had hidden there safely the previous night was missing. He searched for it frantically, and asked everyone in his coach including the Pathan who had been sitting next to him. There was no sign of the note. He started crying aloud, inconsolably.

This was no ordinary 10-rupee note. The year was 1944, and this was the first wage he had received in his own hands. Since his father's death in 1942, he had been working in shops, mainly sweeping, cleaning, and offering water to customers. But he never received the salary he had been promised—Rs 10 to 20 a month; it always went to his elder brothers. In 1944, his brother-in-law's cloth shop in Amritsar, where he was working, closed down. So they sent him back to Karachi, his hometown. As he boarded the train, his brother-in-law gave him that 10-rupee note. Pralhad was so excited that he took it out several times during the day, examined every part of it lovingly like a treasure, and put it back in his kurta pocket. He hid it in his pyjama pocket before going to sleep.

The boy's wailings brought the ticket collector to the scene. He felt sorry for the boy when he heard the story, but said he couldn't do anything to bring the money back. 'It is pointless questioning and searching your fellow passengers,' he added. 'There are so many people in the coach, and everyone could be carrying 10-rupee notes. How would we know which one is yours?' He started to move on as nothing could be done.

'We will know,' said Pralhad emphatically. 'I can tell you the number on my note!' The ticket collector noted down the number in disbelief and asked him if he suspected anyone. Pralhad pointed to the Pathan who had been right next to him throughout the night when he was fast asleep. When questioned by the ticket collector, the Pathan said he had no idea. He was then searched. They found a 10-rupee note in his pugdi. Its number was the same as the one Pralhad had given to the ticket collector.

Adapted from Pralhad P. Chhabria, *There's No Such Thing as a Self-Made Man*, 2008. Pune: Ulhas Chintamani Latkar. Pralhad P. Chhabria is the chairman of the FINOLEX Group.

Know your product or service

Being highly knowledgeable about the product or service that you are selling is important to sustain any good first impression you may have made on the audience. You may not know all the fine technical details if you are, let's say, a sales manager and so not expected to know them; but you should know very well what benefits the product or service will give the customer. You should also have enough understanding of the technical details for you to answer the most common questions potential customers ask.

Work on the audience's emotions

The first step towards enlisting the help of the audience's emotions is to believe that they play an important role in persuasion. We often forget it in the corporate context assuming naïvely that logic and detailed data are what corporate audiences look for. Of course you need data and evidence for you to persuade a corporate audience, but your presentations may fail if you focus on information alone and ignore the role of emotions in disposing the audience favourably towards your proposal.

We shall deal with pathos in our section on delivering the speech.

THE ICEBERG: ADVANCE STRATEGIC PLANNING

The entire discussion in this chapter and the next is based on the firm assumption that persuasion takes place only when the client perceives, rightly or wrongly, that accepting the proposal is good for her. In other words, the proposal is framed in such a way that the prospect perceives it as matching her needs, priorities, and limitations. If she loses something by accepting the proposal, she has to get or hope to get something that more than compensates for that loss. If she does not perceive either a short term or at least a long-term benefit in accepting the proposal, she will not be persuaded. If she complies, it will be because of coercion, not persuasion.

Here is an example. Imagine that you are the managing director of a company faced with a sudden and unusual cash crunch because of an unexpected import-related problem. For various technical reasons you are unable to raise money from commercial banks. You expect the crisis to pass in about three months, when there will be a financial bonanza. You hit upon an idea. Why not divert the money set aside for employee salaries and pensions? Why not borrow additional funds from the employees? How would you sell this idea to them?

Obviously, employees resent any delay in receiving their salary because most of them depend exclusively on it for their regular expenses. Delay hurts their creditworthiness because they will not be able to settle many of the bills they may have run up during the month. If, however, you tell them that the company urgently needs the money and that for the salary that is held back and any additional deposits they make, they will get interest at the rate of 3 percent per month in three months, they may be willing to help out the company. They may have to borrow from friends and other informal sources to survive, but when they realize that they will get an excellent return on their money along with your deep gratitude, most of them will be persuaded to accept your proposal. Of course this assumes that they consider you trustworthy.

Appropriate framing requires strategic planning, which is nothing but figuring out what will work best with the target's decision-making style, and identifying alternative strategies if the preferred strategy does not work as anticipated. After all when we deal with human beings we cannot predict accurately how they will respond to our moves. Something that we think will please them may leave them cold or even antagonistic. They may take seriously a detail that we consider unimportant or even overlook. This is particularly true when we have to deal with a diverse audience. The advantage in the oral medium is that there is generally room for manoeuvre; we can switch to Plan B if we find Plan A running into rough weather, especially if the context is not too formal. Of course switching to Plan B or Plan C assumes that we have Plan B and Plan C in place. This is advance strategic planning (see box, Offence—the Best Defence).

OFFENCE—THE BEST DEFENCE

Shantanurao Kirloskar, the man behind the phenomenal growth of the Kirloskar group, started a joint-venture in 1962 with Cummins Engine Company of Columbus, Indiana, US. In his autobiography, *Cactus & Roses,* he recalls that Kirloskar Cummins Limited (KCL) had several teething problems. The engineers and inspectors that Cummins had sent to help were unhappy with the quality of certain items such as cylinder-liners that KCL produced. They judged that KCL would not be able to make those parts although Kirloskar was quite confident about the ability of his Indian engineers. The relationship between the two was somewhat uneasy. So he decided to go to the Cummins headquarters to sort things out.

Having received reports from their own engineers, the managers there said that KCL should probably be sold to Rolls Royce or some other company that was making large engines like Cummins.

Kirloskar realized that they had lost faith in KCL's ability to make engines to Cummins' specifications and match the quality in their American plant. He did not welcome the suggestion but figured out that Cummins was worried about their investment. So after some more discussion, Kirloskar startled them by saying, 'The Company bears my name—Kirloskar—and I am not selling it. But if Cummins feel that their investment should be recovered, I am willing to buy all Cummins' shares.' They did not have a ready response. They said they would respond the following morning.

When they met the following morning, the Cummins men told Kirloskar that they had decided not to sell their shares to him or to anyone else. They had decided to rely on him because they were impressed by his confidence and were sure that he would succeed.

Source: S.L. Kirloskar, *Cactus & Roses: An Autobiography*, 2003. Pune: Macmillan, pp. 290–1.

As there is no entry barrier to speaking, we are tempted to jump into the arena without checking whether we are ready for it. This is a recipe for disaster. We may or may not succeed in our persuasion attempts. When we fail, we're sad but we don't know why we failed; when we succeed, we are glad but don't know why we succeeded. At times, the target makes a completely unanticipated move and we are forced to retreat well before we have had our say. This is because we get into battle without any strategy whatsoever. Then we depend on luck. But managers ought to do better than that.

Your presentation is like an iceberg. The visible or audible part may be just five to ten minutes. What makes it powerful and successful is the invisible, inaudible part—advance strategic planning.

Advance planning is deciding in advance what to say in what sequence when you meet the prospect. Stated so it appears to be simple, but it isn't. It consists of understanding the client and framing your proposal in such a way that it meets her expectations. She might, for example, expect benefits to be presented in quantitative terms. She might expect a live demonstration. She might want information about and recommendations from existing clients. She may not want to 'waste' her time on technical details; she might want to know how your product or service will help her solve her problems. Or she might be keen to understand the technical details. If you want to persuade her, you need to meet her expectations.

Tips for a strategic plan

Study the context carefully

You must study the context carefully and decide what combination of the several persuasive techniques we identified in Chapter 2 is most appropriate for a given audience. Apart from making yourself likeable and perhaps subtly stroking the target's ego, what techniques should you invest in? Should you, for example, mainly appeal to shared values or play on the audience's herd instinct? Should you leverage any authority you may have and take an assertive line or should you engage the audience in consultation? Should you be content with getting small commitments and build on it for future persuasion efforts? Should you make them indebted to you and dispose them favourably towards your products or services?

The right answer is dynamic; it will depend on the complex relationships between you, your product or service, your audience, and the environment. They may not, for example, be empowered to take a decision even if they accept your proposal. Or, one of your rivals may have made an offer that is clearly superior to yours and, therefore, they are less interested in your proposal. If you are speaking against the backdrop of a crisis, the absence of the luxury of time may prod them into a quick decision. If there are signs that the crisis will blow over, perhaps the audience will be less keen on reaching a decision. Flexibility is thus essential, because in spite of thorough advance planning you may find the client responding differently from what you anticipate.

Frame your proposal cleverly

Clever framing often stands between success and failure in persuasion. Many people who are reluctant to spend Rs 3,500 as annual premium for medical insurance for the whole family on the ground that they can't afford it may be willing to go along if you tell them that for as little as the price of a cup of tea a day, they can insure themselves and their families for a whole year for medical expenses up to Rs 400,000.

GETTING TO YES

Mukesh Ambani was keen on hiring A.G. Dawda, who was doing very well at a Saudi Arabian petrochemical company. The Reliance Petroleum manager who was entrusted with the job of bringing Dawda on board telephoned him, told him about Ambani's interest in him, and asked him if he would consider joining Reliance. The answer was a firm no. Obviously, Dawda saw nothing special in Reliance that would tempt him to give up his job with the Saudi company.

'Come and take a look, and then you can say no,' pleaded the manager. Without waiting for Dawda to confirm that he would be willing to visit the Reliance plant at Jamnagar, the manager sent him a flight ticket. Dawda found it amusing that Reliance was blowing money on a guy who had made it clear that he would not join them! But now that he had no excuse, he flew down.

When he reached Jamnagar, the Reliance manager asked him to drive around to get a feel of the place. Dawda rolled his eyes in disbelief and said to himself: 'Oh God, what do they think they can show a guy who has worked for forty years in the construction industry?' But to humour the manager, Dawda agreed. He drove around. He saw 45,000 people working. After forty-five minutes, he asked the driver to stop. He went to the nearest phone and called Mukesh Ambani in Mumbai and said: 'This is it! The answer is yes.'
Source: Based on an account by Daljit Kaur Gaba, Soma Kolay, and Arti Agnihotri, (eds),. *Rags to Riches: Life & Times of Dhirajlal Hirachand Ambani,* 2002. New Delhi: Pentagon Paperbacks, p. 35.

Follow the top–down approach

In an oral presentation intended to persuade a client, you must generally follow the top-down approach. That is, you must help her perceive the benefits for her almost at the start. If you don't do so, you may lose her. This is because talking takes place in time; she can get your ideas only when you mention them. If you take too long to come to the benefits she gets from accepting your proposal, she may not have the patience to stick with you.

Follow a logical sequence

It is impossible to talk in the abstract about the right sequence for an oral presentation. What we can say is that your presentation should have a smooth structure that helps the audience follow your ideas without any jerks. Chronological, spatial, and cause-and-effect sequences, however, are unlikely to work well. You must start with something that attracts the audience's attention. In the first few minutes, you will do well to demonstrate your understanding of the audience's needs rather than get into self-advertisement. Clients may lose interest in you if you do not quickly come to the point: how your product or service will solve their problem or meet their requirements. Similarly, you need a crisp, powerful ending.

Get your presentation's length right

Whatever the techniques of persuasion you employ, you must make sure that the content of your presentation is neither too long nor too detailed. Faced with detailed content most members of your audience will switch off. An oral presentation is not the best means of presenting detailed information. Your objective as the speaker should be to arouse the audience's interest in your key proposal and to get them to ask you questions. During your talk, don't create a rival for your attention by distributing handouts with detailed information! Consider giving them out at the end of the talk.

DELIVERING THE PERSUASIVE SPEECH

To persuade an audience you must first build rapport with its members. You need to combine two things to achieve it.

▶ **How you connect:** Say something that genuinely pleases the audience. It could be a pat on their back, an expression of joy at being with them, a confession, or anything that helps you connect with them. This is part of your strategic planning of the content of presentation.
▶ **Self-presentation:** Your body language and other non-verbal behaviour should be pleasant, lively, and respectful at the same time. The audience must feel that you belong there. If you are arrogant, they resent it. If you are dull and don't enjoy being there, they get bored and switch off.

> 'When I was a young man, I sold vacuums door-to-door…when [the lady of the house] opened the door, I had to look professional. If I wore my leather jacket, she might have thought I was a hoodlum. In addition, I was told never to sell vacuums in a neighbourhood that doesn't have carpets.'
>
> *Source:* Jerry Della Femina CEO, Della Femina, Rothschild, Jeary, and Partners. Taken from Carol Super (2004). *Selling (without selling)*. New York: Amacom, p. 39.

There are aspects of your non-verbal behaviour that you can control or modify and certain aspects which you cannot change. You can, for example, decide on the kind of clothes to wear when you meet someone or make a public presentation. If your clothes are too formal for the occasion, you put the audience off. If they are too casual for the occasion, you still put the audience off. Similarly, you can decide how formal or informal your behaviour should be based on your relationship with the audience and the context in which you are talking to them.

There are aspects of non-verbal behaviour which you can do little about. The quality of your voice, for example. The effectiveness of your oral persuasion attempt depends to some extent on it. The richer your voice, the more persuasive you are likely to be. Richard Greene, a public-speaking coach, said during a presentation at the 11th Wharton leadership conference, 'I would rather hear Martin Luther King read the Philadelphia White Pages out loud than hear almost anyone in corporate America deliver the "I have a dream" speech.' He was referring to Martin Luther King's celebrated ability to stir feelings in his listeners by the artful use of his voice. A great voice, like some other positive natural attributes, is a gift. If you don't have it, you may have compensating characteristics. Instead of worrying yourself about what you don't have, you should be building on and refining what you do have.

Well meaning public speaking coaches often alert us to the impact the speaker's body language has on the audience and advise speakers to adopt certain types of non-verbal behaviour so that they appear confident and knowledgeable. While the importance of body language is indisputable, this advice may be misplaced. The reason is that the first step towards enhancing your ethos is to be authentic. Be yourself. It is easy for your audience to figure out if you are phony, if you are pretending to be someone or something that you are not. Even if you are very good at pretending, you may find that you slip up when you least expect it. Such failures usually occur when you become emotionally disturbed or when you lower your guard momentarily.

A SMILE CAN LAND YOU IN JAIL!

S.P.S. Rathore, the retired Haryana Director General of Police, was sentenced in December 2009 to six months' rigorous imprisonment for molesting a young girl in 1989. Using his power and political connections he had successfully thwarted for twenty years all attempts to bring him to justice. He appealed against the conviction and asked the Sessions Court for bail. He got it immediately. As he walked out of the court without spending even an hour in jail, there was a smile on his face. This was splashed across the country by the print and electronic media. The smirk angered the public. Everyone took it to mean that he was telling the whole country that no one could touch him.

The judiciary also appears to have taken his smirk seriously. When his appeal against the six-month sentence was disposed of, he was given eighteen months in prison, and was jailed. As *The Times of India* reported on May 25, 2010, the smirk was now gone from Rathore's face.

Press Trust of India reported on May 20, 2010 (*DNA*, Ahmedabad edition) that the Dubai court denied bail to an Indian driver and ordered his arrest because he was found laughing while denying the charge of groping an 18-year old Egyptian housemaid.

A smile can launch a thousand ships; it can also land you in jail.

Whatever your height, weight, figure, complexion, or voice quality, nothing stops you from being pleasant and from being passionate about your proposal. Passion helps you overcome many difficulties including nervousness that you face when you speak to persuade. When you believe passionately in your product or service, you will want to talk about it rather than make a presentation. It will help you adopt a warm conversational style rather than read aloud the text of a speech or the text on PowerPoint slides. Everyone can talk animatedly about things they believe in but few can read aloud with warmth and excitement. When you adopt the conversational style, your voice automatically modulates itself; your pitch and speed of delivery vary according to the emotions displayed; you gesture freely. As Constance Bernstein's research (1994) indicates, 'people who use gestures more freely are more persuasive.' Audiences enjoy such speech and are swayed by it. Perhaps all these signal self-confidence, and audiences love speakers who are confident.

When you talk rather than make a presentation, it is easy for you to establish eye-to-eye contact with members of the audience because that is what you do when you talk to people. The eye contact coupled with a conversational style creates a bond between you and them. This is important because the audience consists of individual human beings made up of flesh and blood. As Chris Segrin, who analysed several research studies, notes, eye contact leads to greater compliance than its absence or avoidance.

Humour, especially of the self-deprecating type, can endear you to your audience. So can memorable metaphors and stories which give very powerful visual support for the points you make.

These, however, have to be used carefully. Your equation with the audience is an important factor in deciding whether humour, picturesque language, and stories are appropriate. You must do everything in your power to grab the audience's attention and retain it.

'He who wants to persuade should put his trust not in the right argument, but in the right word. The power of sound has always been greater than the power of sense.'

—Joseph Conrad, *Lord Jim*, 1900.

If the speech or presentation is very important, it is good to have a rehearsal or two. It is pointless to do it in front of a mirror because your reflection can't be your audience. You can't connect with it. What you really need to check is whether you can connect with people and reach out to them. So the rehearsal should be in front of people. They could be your colleagues or subordinates, provided they are not members of your own team helping you plan the presentation. From such a rehearsal you can learn many things including the time you take, the clarity you have about the issues, and the level of persuasive power you demonstrate. If you want to find out what you look like when you make a speech or a presentation, you should get yourself videographed at the rehearsal rather than deliver a talk to a full-length mirror.

While rehearsing is a good idea, too many rehearsals will spoil your presentation by destroying spontaneity. When you rehearse many times, you almost sound like reciting something you have learnt by heart rather than talking from your heart. The vulnerability associated with spontaneity is more persuasive in a speech or presentation than the flawlessness achieved through repeated practice. This is because spontaneity generally reflects sincerity and guilelessness, which is what an audience will be looking for in a speaker.

DEALING WITH QUESTIONS

Questions from the audience form the heart of a presentation. This is where members of the audience give you a peep into any lingering resistance they may have to your proposal. If you answer them satisfactorily, you remove or, at least, dilute the resistance further and pave the way for them to accept your proposal.

Assume that you are a hawker. You sell leather belts from a cart. A man finds a particular leather belt attractive. He asks you for the price. You quote a figure. He says he doesn't want the belt because the price is too high. You then ask him to quote a price that he thinks is reasonable. He does. Although it gives you a good profit, you say that the price is too low and you will lose money if you sell the belt at that price. He, however, insists that he is not at all interested in the belt except at that price. You finally agree to that price. Now he cannot walk away without buying the belt. He is honour-bound to buy because you have agreed to the price that he himself had quoted. In the same way, your audience is honour-bound to accept your product, service, or idea once you answer all their questions satisfactorily.

When you plan the presentation, you base your strategy on your understanding of the client's needs, priorities, and limitations. You may have gone wrong in your analysis or underestimated their resistance. Clients may not always make clear exactly what they want or what considerations will govern their buying decisions. Besides, there may be some unexpected members joining the audience. Questions from the audience during or after your presentation point to their real worries and priorities. If you can anticipate them and go prepared with answers that will satisfy them, you are likely to succeed in your persuasion attempt.

There is, of course, the possibility that the client also takes a strategic approach. He may have already decided not to buy your product or service; he may ask you questions to merely keep you engaged or to lead you on. He may raise questions which do not reflect his real needs or real resistance to your proposal. You will need to distinguish between genuine questions and fake ones. It is your experience and advance strategic planning that should help you deal appropriately with this.

In her book, *Selling (without selling)*, Carol Super summarizes one such experience (pp. 114–15). It is narrated by Rob Reif, her young associate. He had accompanied Carol for a meeting with an important prospect. The meeting came to a point where the client asked her whether she could run some numbers on ten markets. Rob thought that it was great and would have eagerly agreed to get the numbers and bag the order. He was, therefore, shocked to hear Carol say: 'I can see that you're not ready to buy right now. Whenever you are, please call me and I'll give you any information you need.' Rob adds that Carol could recognize what he calls the 'stop sign' here. The client was not interested in those numbers; she was merely being nice to them and making them feel that their trip was not wasted.

The advantage of getting into the question and answer mode is that you leave the one-way monologue for the two-way dialogue, which is invariably livelier and more focused on the members of the audience. Even those who deliver presentations in a monotonous voice and with poor eye contact become animated and fully engaged when they start answering questions from the audience. If members of the audience start asking you questions during your presentation, you should be prepared to set your planned presentation aside and answer them. This is, of course, tougher than delivering a well ordered presentation without any interruption. There is also the risk of the audience losing the thread of your argument. If you have mastered the content, you should be able to slice it up and offer it in response to questions without sacrificing coherence. After all, you achieve your objective when you engage the audience, not when you merely deliver a flawless presentation.

In spite of the critical importance of dealing with questions, this is one area that is ignored by many speakers, even those who invest time and effort in elaborately planning their presentations. Their preparation does not take into account the kind of questions that might come from the audience. As a result, regardless of a well-delivered presentation they may end up looking incompetent because they are unable to answer some questions from the audience. The rehearsal that we talked about above should also have a question and answer component. You should encourage your audience at the rehearsal to ask you tough questions so that you are prepared fully for questions that come from the real audience.

A DEVIL'S ADVOCATE

The next time you rehearse an important presentation in front of a few colleagues, ask one of them in advance to be the devil's advocate. Ask him or her to be somewhat obstructive and very difficult to please. See how you cope with someone who is not impressed by your ideas or arguments. See where you have no answers to the objections that they raise or where you have no arguments to counter theirs. Working with such a sparring partner may be your best preparation for a difficult presentation.

If you make a team presentation, it is essential to organize at least a couple of rehearsals where you respond to questions from a pretend-audience. You will then be able to decide who should field what kind of questions. You can also test the quality of coordination within the team. Quite a few team presentations are spoilt at the question-and-answer time because team members don't agree among themselves or because two or more members try to answer questions at the same time.

Even after thorough preparation, you may find yourself unable to cope with certain questions from the audience because you don't have the right answers. You must resist the temptation to bluff the audience. It is best to admit that you don't know the answer and promise to provide it later. If you make such a promise, you must keep it.

THE TECHNOLOGY CHALLENGE

Technology helps you reach out effortlessly to ever larger audiences at multiple locations across the globe. Technology gives you tools to create strikingly powerful visual aids that will make your presentations more appealing. A well-made PowerPoint presentation with additional inputs such as video clips reassures the audience that you are well prepared. This is an important consideration because no audience likes to be taken for granted. Corporate audiences are likely to be easily put off by speakers who ramble on with no evidence of homework done.

But technology is no unmixed blessing. While it dazzles, it can also stand between you and the audience. We have already noted that ethos and pathos are far more important than logos in oral persuasion. But technology can grow big and dwarf the speaker. We often find slick PowerPoint presentations with bells and whistles where the speaker is little more than a mouse-clicker. This is no way to reach out to the audience, connect with it, and influence it favourably towards you and your product, service, or idea.

Some speakers become so dependent on technology that they are unable to speak to a group of people without hanging on to PowerPoint slides. They are like doctors who can't diagnose even jaundice until all the laboratory test results are in. Such slavish dependence on technology takes away spontaneity and warmth, which are great assets for a persuader.

Technology can also make persuasive communication harder by taking away some of the clues your audience usually gives you. When you have a teleconference, for example, you can speak to several people simultaneously although they are in different parts of the world. You, however, have access only to their voices. In the absence of visual clues, you may find it difficult to interpret their message. Even a video conference is not quite the same thing as a regular, face-to-face meeting. Technology stretches the possibilities in one direction even as it shrinks them in another.

CONCLUSION

To become a persuasive speaker you need to enhance your ethos: your credibility, expertise, and trustworthiness. Advance strategic planning is essential if you want to frame your proposal to match the needs, priorities, and limitations of your target audience. Whether you try to persuade one or many, you must arouse their emotions in your favour through the way you deliver your speech. The most important qualities of persuasive delivery are self-confidence and passion. You need logic to be persuasive, but it will work only when your target has been disposed favourably towards you through the other two persuasion factors.

LESSONS LEARNT

- ▶ Whether you speak or write, the basic principles of persuasion are the same. There are, however, major differences in the way the two mediums influence the target.
- ▶ Ethos and pathos are more important than logos in oral persuasion.
- ▶ If your persuadees perceive you as likeable, credible, knowledgeable, fair-minded, and trustworthy, your proposal has a very good chance of being accepted.
- ▶ Persuasion takes place only when the client perceives, rightly or wrongly, that accepting your proposal is good for her. Give her this reassurance early in your speech.
- ▶ To persuade an audience you must first build rapport with the members through right words and right non-verbal behaviour.
- ▶ Be authentic. Be passionate about what you propose. You will be persuasive.
- ▶ Figure out your audience's real resistance to your ideas by paying attention to the questions they ask.
- ▶ Use technology to maximize the benefits of using the oral medium, but be aware of its limitations.

In this chapter we have dwelt on persuasion through the spoken medium. In the next chapter we shall focus on the written medium. We shall identify the steps we need to take if we decide to persuade someone through writing.

REFERENCES

Bernstein, C. (1994). 'Winning Trials Nonverbally: Six Ways to Establish Control in the Courtroom'. *Trial*, vol. 30, pp. 61–5.

Greene, R. (2007). Secrets of Public Speaking. http://www.management today.co.uk/channel/MarketingSales/news/734598/ (last accessed on May 20, 2010).

Segrin, C. (1993). 'The effects of Nonverbal Behavior on Outcomes of Compliance Gaining Attempts'. *Communication Studies*, vol. 44, pp. 169–87.

Super, C. (2004). *Selling (Without Selling)*. New York: Amacom, pp. 114–15.

8

The Persuasive Writer

INTRODUCTION

Writers, we have noted in Chapter 7, are from Mount Everest. It is much harder to get anywhere near Mount Everest than to head to a sunny, sandy beach. Writing requires as much rigorous training and discipline as mountaineering because writers are made, not born. Nonetheless, it is worth developing persuasive writing. It is invaluable in many contexts where you cannot use the spoken medium at all and in certain other contexts where writing is much more efficient a medium than speaking.

Persuasive writing is not just for advertisers and sales managers. Every manager needs it. The need to persuade through writing has grown considerably in recent years in the wake of the growing popularity of e-mail for regular internal and external communication. We will therefore not focus here on the copy that advertisers write or special letters that sales managers and direct marketers write to sell products and services to external customers. We can, of course, learn from the fascinating work they do, but we shall focus mainly on the persuasive writing managers employ when they draft internal and external e-mail messages, letters, proposals, and reports. You may not make it to

Mount Everest, but you can scale lower peaks if you master, or at least attempt to master, the basic techniques of persuasion.

As we have already noted, persuasion can be both oral and written. The three persuasion factors—ethos, pathos, and logos—are equally relevant although logos tends to receive greater weight when the medium is written. The persuasive strategies that we have highlighted in our relationships with bosses, peers, subordinates, and customers are relevant as well. Therefore, in this chapter, we shall focus on identifying the advantages and disadvantages of the written medium for persuasion and figuring out ways of overcoming the various disadvantages while building on the advantages.

DISADVANTAGES OF WRITING

If you are a peacock and want to draw the attention of the peahens in your neighbourhood, you can fly over to where they are gossiping, spread your glorious wings, and strut around. They may or may not display any interest in you, but they are sure to notice you. What can you do if you are a wildflower in a desert and desperately want to attract certain types of insects to help you with pollination? You can't go over to places where those insects congregate. So you try other tricks. You don brilliant colours or spread alluring scents to draw them to you. You make it difficult for insects to ignore you.

If you are a writer, you have a lot in common with the wildflower. You are denied many of the liberties a speaker enjoys to draw her listener's attention. You have no control over the reader. He may miss your e-mail among the dozens of messages that pile up in his inbox every hour. He may notice it, but choose to skip it nonetheless. He may open it, read a paragraph or two, and ignore the rest because he may think that he has got the complete message. He may misunderstand one or two expressions in your mail and arrive at unanticipated conclusions in the absence of anyone to correct him. He may read it, but not with the thoroughness you expect, and so miss out on some of the critical points you make.

Even if he reads and understands what you have written, he may think that it does not concern him and ignore the message. You may not be aware that your message has been brushed aside because you failed to frame the issue in a way that would make it appear relevant to him. Similarly, he may read it and reject your proposal because it may raise some objections in his mind as he reads it. Some of these may be trivial and you can easily refute them if he shares them with you. But he does not, because you are not around when he reads your document. In short, writing is dead-end communication; you don't get a chance to re-frame or recast your idea, which you normally get as a speaker. If he is an internal customer and writes back to let you know that he does not accept your proposal, you may still not know why. If he gives reasons for his rejection, they may be politically correct statements rather than genuine explanations. If he responds with silence to your written proposal, you wouldn't know whether he has read it and rejected it or whether he is yet to read it.

Persuasion through writing faces yet another challenge: the possibility of being subjected to severe criticism. Unlike a listener who may have to respond almost instantly to an orally presented proposal, your reader generally gets enough time to analyse your document thoroughly. He can re-read it several times if he wishes to. If he does not understand it fully or does not trust you, he can take the help of an expert and decide whether to accept your proposal or not. Thus, your document may be subjected to more intense scrutiny than an oral presentation.

While writers have to gear up to face extreme criticism, they are increasingly faced with an additional and diametrically opposite challenge—hurried, shallow reading. There was a time when you could expect your target readers to read your documents in the comfort of their offices or homes. Now you cannot anticipate the conditions under which they will access your document. Some may read it on their laptops or desktops in their office; some may read it on their handhelds while queuing up to board a flight or waiting for the traffic light to turn green. Those who access your message on the road may not be able to give your document the attention you believe it deserves.

Unlike speaking, which children pick up effortlessly and with joy, writing is a difficult, cultivated skill. Because it is difficult, many managers avoid practising it and make it even harder for them to develop persuasive written documents.

ADVANTAGES OF WRITING

In spite of such serious weaknesses, writing has substantial strengths as a persuasive medium that more than make up for them.

The greatest advantage is that you can separate yourself from your documents in time and space. This allows you to sell products, services, and ideas to people you cannot approach directly and people who are in different time zones. The documents you generate, if well designed, will do the job for you round the clock without any geographic restrictions. You can write when you find it convenient to write; the readers can read when they find it convenient to read. In a sense, writing affords you a certain degree of omnipresence. This is particularly relevant if you want to persuade your super bosses several rungs above you in the office hierarchy or bosses and colleagues who are geographically distanced from you.

Another major advantage with writing is that you can do it in the comfort of your office or home, away from the pressure of an audience sitting in front of you. Even if you are well prepared for a speech or a conversation, you can be unsettled by the presence of certain people in the audience or the way they ask you questions or respond to you. This may thwart your persuasion attempts although you have all the information required. With one-on-one-meetings also you may become tongue-tied if the person you have to persuade is intimidating. When you write, you don't have such pressures although anyone could experience 'writer's block' even in a relaxed state of mind. After all, writing is a difficult skill. However, you do have the advantage of getting others to help review your text, improve it, and make it stand up to most extreme forms of criticisms.

The discipline of writing forces you to think many ideas through. You may be able to get away with vague or unclear statements when you speak, but not when you write. You cannot expect any help from the reader through requests for clarifications. If you don't present your ideas clearly, you will put the reader off; you may even lose her. If some members of your audience switch off, you can sense it. You will, however, never know when your readers switch off. You have to anticipate such problems well in advance and take preventive measures. Your efforts to do that will save you from woolly thinking and half-baked ideas. Nearly five centuries ago, English author and philosopher Sir Francis Bacon brilliantly captured this advantage of writing, 'Reading maketh a full man, conference a ready man, and writing an exact man.'

If your proposal is a major one that requires the support of a variety of data and evidence, writing may be the only reasonable channel to persuade others to study it carefully and to accept it.

It is rarely that a company takes a major decision based exclusively on an oral presentation. Even if the CEO of a company takes a decision based on an oral pitch or on impulse, she would nonetheless want a written document that will sell the idea to others in the organization and serve as a record.

HOW TO OVERCOME THE CHALLENGE OF WRITING

If the ability to persuade through writing is not just useful but almost essential in the corporate world, we need to figure out how to overcome the disadvantages of the medium and maximize its advantages. We shall look at a few ways here.

Capture the Reader's Attention Quickly

If you want to be a persuasive writer, the first step is to draw the elusive reader's attention. Here we can learn a lot from billboard advertisers. They have to attract motorists or pedestrians going about their business. Billboards can't shout. They can't stretch a hand out and beckon anyone. Therefore, billboard advertisers do four things to draw our attention and to make us read their story:

▶ Whenever possible, they set up billboards at strategic locations, spots where your eyes go without any special prompting.
▶ They display on these hoardings something striking, for example, a pretty face, the familiar face of a popular politician or film star.
▶ They use just a few words to tell a story that intrigues you or caters to your needs.

▶ They use large and simple fonts so that you can read and understand the main story in a second or two, without having to stop the car or to go near the hoarding.

You have to follow broadly the same philosophy to capture your reader's attention. The title of a report and the subject line of an e-mail or a letter are the strategic spots to which the reader's eyes go first. You have to make sure that the title or the subject line is attractive and to the point, but not flippant. A well-crafted title not only tells the reader about what content she can expect, but also about what kind of quality she can anticipate in the e-mail or letter. It can also signal the framing you have adopted to make your message persuasive. Even a busy reader should be able to figure out from the subject line that the text is relevant and that he should read on.

An intriguing subject line is likely to arouse the reader's curiosity or stimulate some of his instincts. Here we should learn from spammers. Some of the subject lines they use are so attractive that it is difficult not to click open the mail. Few people can, for example, resist:

Congratulations! You've just won US$5.28 million!
Winner's notification
Missing child
Virus alert

You haven't bought any lottery ticket or entered any competition. Your child is safe at home. You don't know of any friends or acquaintances whose child is missing. Still, you are intrigued. You are constantly worried about your computer's safety. So if there is a new virus lurking in the neighbourhood, you want to know about it immediately and prevent it. The subject line hooks you; you click the mail open.

A lazy title like 'Report' or e-mail subject line such as 'hi' or 'request' may not arouse the reader's interest. She may ignore it unless her job requires her to read written communications from you. Even in such contexts where the reader is almost guaranteed to pay attention, a brief but descriptive title such as 'analysis of recent boiler room accident' (in place of 'report' or 'accident') and 'Can we meet 3 pm tomorrow, December 17?' (in place of 'meeting' or 'meeting of the subcommittee for review of innovative sales practices in rural and semi-urban areas') is likely to be more attractive and informative. Some writers deny themselves the opportunity to attract the reader and frame the contents by leaving the subject line blank.

Of course, letters and e-mail from friends and relations belong to an entirely different category. What is most attractive in them is not the subject line but the sender's name. We will read *any mail* from them whether there is a subject line or not.

Get the Body Language Right

It is well known that we are influenced by the body language of the people we interact with. Their facial expressions, gestures, posture, attire, and other aspects of their appearance subtly and subconsciously influence our responses to them. One aspect of writing is that the author's body language is irrelevant. There is, however, another body language that influences the reader: the presentation of your document.

If your text appears on paper, the quality of stationery and printing can quickly lead the reader to certain conclusions, some unfair, about the quality of the report or letter on it. Electronic communication has given us a more level-playing field. There is still no escape from the influence of physical appearance. The spelling, the layout, and the choice of font can all influence the reader positively or negatively. How would you, for instance, respond to the following mail if you were the senior manager for maintenance at your company's headquarters in Mumbai and you received it? The mail is from the plant-engineering department in your factory in Andhra Pradesh. (This e-mail is reproduced without any change whatsoever, except the writer's name.)

Subject: PROBLEMS IN NITROGEN PLANT

DEAR SIR
UR ALRDY AWARE THAT THE NITRO PLANT IS HAVING PRBLMS IN OPS. IT IS TAKING 10-12 HRS TO DVLP 4KG/SQCM PRESSURE AND THE TIMER FR PRESSURE SWING AJSTMENT UNITS ARE SOME TIMES NOT WORKING PRPRLY, CAUSE OF WHICH THE FLOW ITSELF IS NOT CONTINUOUS. WE HAVE RGD A CMPLNT TO THE LOCAL off about this prblm one month back and their srvc engr is yet to attend the same. we are told that there is only one srvc engr and he has to take care of total ap inspite of our regular reminders over phone about the prblm to them they have not taken any action on this matter. hence you pls contact their ho and ask them to arrange some one asap.
regards
ram lakhan

In spite of the annoyance you feel, you may take the trouble of deciphering this e-mail and responding because it is from your own organization. If, however, it comes from an external source or someone you don't know, you are likely to ignore it. In either case, the e-mail does not create a good, favourable impression in your mind about the writer. A little improvement in the layout, combined with better sentence construction, could have made the e-mail more persuasive.

Subject: Urgent need for Service Engineer in Nitrogen Plant

Dear Mr Mankarkar [or 'Sir,' if that is what the company culture demands]

As you know, the Nitrogen plant has been running inefficiently.

▶ It takes 10-12 hrs to build up 4 kg/sq cm pressure.

▶ The timer for PSA units is defective (and so the flow is not continuous).

We complained to the supplier's (Acme Enterprises') Hyderabad office a month ago, and have reminded them several times. They have not attended to the problem yet because, apparently, they have just one service engineer for the entire state.

Could you please contact Acme's Head Office at Mumbai and get a service engineer sent here immediately?

Thank you very much
Ram Lakhan

You may think that you don't have time to make your e-mail messages neat and easy to read. Don't be surprised if you save five minutes and then spend fifty minutes in follow-up or explanatory e-mail.

The now common declaration at the bottom of the e-mail, 'Sent from handheld' helps the reader forgive many sins, but if your objective is to persuade someone, especially someone who is not obliged to read and respond to your message, you had better avoid them.

Avoid Obvious Irritants

When you reach out through letters and e-mail to people you have never met, your entire persuasion attempt may come to naught because something in your document annoys them. One of the common irritants is insensitivity to the reader's gender.

Women, for example, are unlikely to enjoy reading a letter or e-mail that starts with the salutation, 'Dear Sir,' or 'Dear Mr Pandit.' Yet, many such offensive letters reach women because their writers do not bother to find out about the gender of the recipient. Even banks and insurance companies, which have all the details of their customers, occasionally annoy their customers, especially women, by not showing enough sensitivity to their gender.

There are of course problem names. Some first names such as 'Kiran' are shared by members of both genders. Some men have names widely associated with women and the other way round (for example, Ananya for men and Pankaj for women). Foreign names also may pose a problem. If the person you are writing to is really important to you, you will want to find out the correct gender and address that person appropriately. If they are not very important, you can get round the problem by using the first and the surname together (Dear Kiran Pandit) or the initials and the surname together (Dear K.L. Pandit) avoiding gender-related titles such as Mr, Ms, or Mrs.

Wrongly spelt personal names can be another major irritant. Some may choose to ignore the violence done to their names by writers of letters and e-mail addressed to them. Notwithstanding this, being casual about the recipients' names is certainly not the best way to influence your readers positively towards your persuasion attempts.

Among the easily avoidable irritants are spelling and grammar errors along with poor punctuation. Some of these errors make it impossible for the reader to figure out the meaning of your message. Many errors may not block comprehension but certainly make it difficult. All of them are likely to irritate the reader and dispose him negatively towards the persuasive message.

Make It Easy for the Reader

As more and more of your readers are likely to access your message under unfavourable conditions far away from their offices, it is important to make the text easy for the reader to process. If you have a complex message to share with your reader, don't rely exclusively on text; supplement it with visual support. If you want to keep your message short, you may be able to supply additional support as attachments that the reader may access only if she needs to.

Except in a technical report, use conversational language because it is easier than formal language. Bureaucratic language can make even simple messages somewhat difficult to retrieve. Here is a simple message from a bank to its customers who have failed to maintain the minimum quarterly average balance in their savings accounts.

> As per the current rules relating to Savings Bank Account, a minimum "Quarterly Average Balance" of Rs._____ is required to be maintained. However, during the last one/two quarter(s), the average balance maintained in your aforesaid account is below the stipulated minimum.
>
> In order to service your account properly, we request you to kindly adhere to, in future, requirement of minimum average balance in your account.

The bank wants to persuade these account holders to maintain the minimum quarterly average balance. Although this is a very short message (just sixty five words), many readers will need to go over the text twice to figure out exactly what is required. Why not make it simpler, like the following?

> We find that the average quarterly balance in your savings account is below Rs ----------, the minimum required.
> Please keep the balance above the minimum and avoid paying extra charges.

Even with the addition of an incentive ('avoid paying extra charges') for the reader to comply with the request, this text uses less than half the words of the original. It is also much easier to read and understand.

Of course, simple, conversational language on its own does not guarantee clarity. Once you decide what ideas you want to present and in what order, you must use language that is appropriate to the content and level of readers.

Choose the Most Effective Sequence

Once you are clear about what you want to communicate, you need to decide on the best sequence to present your ideas in. There are different kinds of sequences, all equally logical, but not equally effective in writing. Often managers are tempted to give detailed background information before they come to the idea they want to sell. This bottom-up approach is perfectly logical, but most likely to fail. The simple reason is that without an objective or a framework the reader cannot make sense of the detailed information you supply. She may wonder why she should plod through it at all and decide that she has better things to do with her time.

If you follow the top-down approach in which you tell the reader up front what you want and then give the corroborating data or evidence, the reader is likely to find it easier to process. If you start with what is in it for him, he is likely to be interested in reading on. If you frame the issue right at the start in such a way that your reader perceives it as relevant and useful, or at least intriguing, there is a very good chance that he will continue reading.

Here is an extract from a full-page letter of invitation the director of PQR College of Management sent to a professor of management (all names changed).

Dear Dr. Parmar ji,

Namaskar.

Stewarded by an eminent governing council embellished by persons of your eminence and steered by management and faculty with acknowledged credentials, PQR College of Management has made a formidable presence in the comity of management academia across the country.

It is PQR's conviction that management education cannot be effectively imparted through the conventional classroom format. It calls for an integrative learning methodology involving purposive and active interaction with the real life business environment. PQR, therefore, lays special accent on expert lectures, case-discussions, business games, industrial visits, etc. Over a period of more than six years, PQR students had the occasion to listen to about 150 experts from within and outside of India.

There is no subject line that tells the reader that this is a letter of invitation. So he wonders why he is subjected to a detailed description of the glories of PQR, which he has never heard of. Perhaps the writer feels that if she does not establish the credentials of her college and impress the reader before inviting him, he may decline the invitation. This is a valid argument, but she is likely to be disappointed because the reader may not even read beyond the first paragraph let alone respond favourably.

The top-down approach is not without problems though. The reader may reject the proposal without even bothering to read the justification that follows. Even if he reads the justification, he may assess it negatively because he has already rejected the conclusion or the proposal. Another problem with the top-down approach is that the reader may not have enough background information to make sense of the conclusion or the proposal.

Thus, there are no universal guidelines on the best sequence that one can routinely follow. You have to decide in each case what would be the best sequence. What is important to realize is that sequence plays an important role in making your ideas accessible to your readers. When you deliberately mould your writing to suit your intended readers, you will also be able to judge reliably what information can be assumed and what information has to be supplied. When you write to persuade, you have to walk a tightrope balancing between boring the reader with unwanted information and puzzling the reader with information gaps.

Anticipate Objections and Deal with Them

We have noted in Chapter 7 that one of the advantages of a speaker trying to persuade an audience is that she can respond to any objections that members of the audience may raise to her proposal. When the objections are dealt with satisfactorily, the audience's resistance melts. If the reader has objections to the proposal you have put in a written text, he may mail back; it is also possible that he rejects the proposal without even letting you know why. He may not read beyond the point where he disagrees with you. In order to get his compliance, you have to anticipate possible objections and deal with them in advance.

When you are convinced about the value of the proposal you are making, it is difficult to anticipate the kind of objections that may arise in your target reader's mind. It is equally difficult to identify expressions that may puzzle the reader. It is a good idea, therefore, to share your text with someone and get it critiqued before you send it out. This is not always practical but you should do it at least in important persuasion attempts to reduce the chances of your target readers misunderstanding or misinterpreting your proposal and rejecting it.

The easiest remedy is to share your text with someone and ask her to read it critically. She may tell you whether your text can withstand criticism from the potential reader. You may be a poor judge of the robustness of your own arguments and the validity of the evidence you present. So if you are writing to persuade a person who is likely to look out for weaknesses in your argument, and if it is important to take him on board, you must get a friend or colleague to vet your text before you send it out to him. The written medium gives you the freedom to do so.

Give the Reader Enough Signposts

In a tiny village you don't find any signposts because you don't need any. You can readily see landmarks such as major buildings. In a large city, however, it is virtually impossible to reach your destination without several signposts. In the same way if your written message is very brief, such as a single-paragraph e-mail, you don't need to invest in providing signposts. An appropriate subject line is all the signposting your reader needs. If it is a longer e-mail, report, or proposal, you have to ensure excellent signposting through appropriate headings and subheadings, numbers, bullets, and highlighting devices such as italicizing, underlining, and boldfacing. If you deal with two distinct items in a single e-mail, you will help the reader if you number the items as 1 and 2. The moment your reader sees 1 prefixed to an item, she knows that there is at least one more item to come even if it is not immediately visible on the screen.

You *must*, of course, guard against excessive signposting. This paragraph illustrates what **not** to do. Some writers use **multiple highlighting devices** such as italics and boldface repeatedly to draw the reader's attention to what they consider *important*. This is likely to **annoy** certain readers who may feel that their *intelligence* is being **insulted**. In any case, that will be **counter-productive** because if you highlight every other sentence or phrase in your letter or e-mail, *nothing* will get the importance it deserves.

Make your Text as Concise as You Can

If you ramble when you speak, your listener can stop you and ask questions. As your reader cannot do so, he may switch off. Obviously, you cannot persuade someone who is not paying attention to you. So come quickly to the point. Don't beat around the bush.

Writing concisely is not at all easy, but nonetheless extremely important in the corporate context. Few managers are willing to read and re-read lengthy texts looking for your meaning hidden away somewhere in them. If your e-mail extends beyond the first screen, you may lose the reader. Besides, they may access your document on a handheld, which is not a good platform for processing long texts.

You cannot write concisely unless you are clear about what you want to communicate. Before you write you must think through the issue so that you know what you want to communicate and how much of it should be articulated in the document. In the absence of clear thinking, you cannot make your writing clear and tight however proficient you may be in the language you use.

Once you know exactly what you want to communicate, imagine your reader sitting across your desk, and write as if you were talking to her. Once you write the text down, go through it again to check if you can cut down a few words. Often we find a lot of flab as we saw in the letter from the bank in the section, Make It Easy for the Reader.

Make Your Text as Graphic as You Can

Try describing a common flower such as hibiscus or marigold without naming it. Don't be surprised if many of your readers cannot identify the flower from your description. Try describing the facial expression of a person displaying pride or contempt without naming the emotion. Don't be surprised if none of your readers identify the emotion correctly. The proverbial picture will do the job far more easily than a thousand words. You need to make your writing graphic if you want to persuade your readers by appealing to their emotions rather than just their reasoning. Well-chosen metaphors and analogies help the reader understand and accept your ideas although they are not proofs.

Here, for instance, is the way a woman writes about her initial self-portrayal on a dating website. She says it is an advertisement to attract a suitable man rather an honest self-portrait. She uses the metaphor of striptease very effectively:

> What I mean is that I start with a full clothed version of me that I put up as an advertisement—makeup and posh frock to get men interested! Then as I write emails and get to know someone I reveal more of the real me and if we both seem to like what we see of each other we might arrange a meeting. If I decide I'm no longer interested I can easily say so and that is the end of it.
>
> *Source:* M. Hardey, 'Life Beyond the Screen: Embodiment and Identity through the Internet'. *The Sociological Review*, 50 (4), 2002, p.578

Of course an analogy does not prove anything. However, it helps the reader perceive things in a particular frame and accept it. Graphic writing tends to be more interesting for readers and is therefore more persuasive.

LEVERAGING LOGOS

Just as in spoken persuasion, credibility is important in written persuasion too. However, the physical separation of the document from the writer tends to shift the focus from the writer's credibility to the quality of reasoning in the document. If you have a reputation for expertise and trustworthiness, your readers are likely to take your proposals seriously and give you the benefit of the doubt if there is a lack of clarity in some parts. If your executive summary is written well and you have a reputation for expertise and integrity, your reader may not scrutinize the whole report. She may accept the findings assuming that the claims you make in the executive summary are adequately supported with reliable data in the report.

You often attempt written persuasion in the upward direction partly because you can't easily approach managers a couple of rungs above you and partly because the document is expected to speak for itself. When your boss forwards it with her recommendation to her boss, the document acquires some credibility. Whether that happens or not, there should be internal credibility, which should come from the kind of data you use and the quality of reasoning you employ.

Within the organization you may write a variety of documents on, for example, launching new products and services, pricing new or existing products and services, and identifying trade partners. These could be proposals and decision reports in which you recommend or justify certain decisions based on your analysis of the situation or of the risks involved, and evaluation of various options. In some reports you may focus on plans versus achievements. You may identify the shortcomings and offer your analysis of their reasons. Logic is the heart of such texts. Your analysis has to be such that the reader has no difficulty going along and accepting your conclusion.

Many managers fail to leverage logos in their reports and proposals because they make untenable claims or claims that they do not support adequately with the right kind of evidence. Here is a claim from a report. Most critical readers would find it difficult to accept it and, as a result, ignore the rest of the argument.

> DoT (Department of Telecommunications) chose 'circles' as the unit for bidding for administrative convenience, hence India was divided into twenty one circles.

The writer is making a cause-and-effect relationship between DoT's choice of 'circles' as the unit for bidding (cause) and division of India into twenty one circles (effect). The real relationship between the two is just the opposite. Since DoT found existing states or districts to be inappropriate as units for bidding, it divided the country into twenty one new units (some the same as an existing state, some part of a large state, and some a clubbing of two or more small states) and treated them as units for bidding. DoT chose to call them 'circles' because the new units did not correspond to any of the existing divisions such as states. DoT could have called them zones or blocks instead of circles; it wouldn't have made any difference.

You can generally get away with such lack of logical rigour when you speak. If someone raises an objection, you can explain your meaning and move on. When your written text fends for itself in the reader's territory, some of these holes appear to be large craters. Readers balk at them. If there are two or three such instances in your written persuasion effort, you may lose a very critical reader.

Another common defect in logical reasoning is attributing an effect to a single cause when it has multiple causes. This is a kind of overstatement, which critical readers resent. You encounter it both in analyses of past events (reports) and projections of future events (plans and proposals). At times, writers do this with fraudulent intentions, as we shall see in Chapter 9. Mostly, however, it is due to the lack of logical rigour in the analysis. Here is an example of attributing the entire effect to one of the several causes.

> We should continue with our television commercials because they led to a 12.73 percent increase in the sale of our detergents during the second half of this year.

The television commercials may have helped the sale of the detergents. If, however, market data show that competitors, some of whom did not advertise, also saw their sales go up by about 10 percent during the same period, we cannot attribute our increase in sales solely to television advertising. If we don't want our enlightened reader to disagree with such claims and discontinue reading, we need to tone our claims down. Here are two ways of making the request more acceptable:

> We should continue with our television commercials because, boosted by them, the sale of our detergents grew by 12.73 percent during the second half of this year.

Or

> We should continue with our television commercials because they appear to have helped the sale of our detergents grow by 12.73 percent during the second half of this year.

CONCLUSION

Persuasive writing is something every manager needs in his day-to-day work life. Its importance has increased along with the remarkable growth of e-mail for official internal and external communication. Many managers do not, however, hone their persuasive writing adequately because it is a difficult, cultivated skill compared to speaking, which is natural and relatively effortless.

The main disadvantage of the writer is that she has no control over the reader who is separated from her in time and space. He may arrive at wrong conclusions either because he does not read the whole document or because he reads it without adequate attention. The main advantage of writing is that it can readily transcend the limitations of time and space on the one hand and hierarchy on the other. It also frees the writer from the kind of pressures that make a speaker tongue-tied in the presence of extremely critical audiences. Honing persuasive writing is useful because there are contexts in which the written medium is more efficient than the spoken medium.

In this chapter, we looked at many ways of overcoming the disadvantages of the written medium and enhancing its use.

Lessons learned

In order to meet the challenge of writing we have to:

- ▶ Capture the reader's attention
- ▶ Get the document's body language right
- ▶ Avoid things that may irritate the reader
- ▶ Make the text easy for the reader
- ▶ Choose the most effective sequence of ideas
- ▶ Anticipate the reader's potential objections and resolve them
- ▶ Give the reader enough signposts
- ▶ Make the text as concise as we can
- ▶ Make the text as graphic as we can

Apart from these, we should also enhance the internal credibility of the document if we want to be persuasive. This stems from the kind of data we use and the quality of reasoning we employ. Logic is the heart of such texts. Our reasoning should be such that the reader has no difficulty going along and accepting our conclusion.

REFERENCE

Hardey, M. (2002). 'Life Beyond the Screen: Embodiment and Identity Through the Internet'. *The Sociological Review*, 50 (4) pp. 570–85.

9

The Ethical Persuader

INTRODUCTION

If you are an ethical persuader, it does not imply that you are a saint or an alien. You are just a manager who follows the norms of fairness when you attempt to persuade others. You compete with others and make money, but you don't sell your products, services, or ideas to others by misleading or deceiving them, that is, by using unfair means such as suppression of critical information or introduction of false information, or both. This is especially so when you hold a position that is generally accepted as a credible source of information or when you deal with people who trust you blindly.

Ethics governs your relationship and interaction with others. It complements law. It does not contradict self-interest but sublimates it. If you are interested in long-term success, you have to be an ethical persuader. You can achieve quick success through deception, but it is likely to be short-lived. Your scope for future growth may be severely restricted if deception is central to your business model.

In this chapter, we shall look at what it means to be an ethical persuader and why it is important for both managers and their organizations to strive towards establishing ethical persuasion as the norm. We shall start with a discussion of ethics. We shall note that the world of ethics is full of ambiguities and uncertainties. Many ethical norms are not necessarily universal but tied to regional cultures.

Business ethics is more problematic because companies and managers within them compete fiercely and are easily tempted to gain an unfair advantage over rivals. However, even in business, it pays to be ethical although it is virtually impossible to define the term. We shall attempt to formulate a few guidelines for ethical persuasion, especially with reference to withholding information from the persuadee. We shall also look at how the leaders of a company can communicate their ethical values to the rest of the organization.

THE MURKY BUSINESS OF ETHICS

In *Ethics Incorporated: Top Priority and Bottom Line*, Dipankar Gupta makes a very useful distinction between 'moral' and 'ethical.' Morality governs your personal beliefs and values; it need not involve others. Ethics governs your relationship and interaction with others. The basis of ethical behaviour is the firm belief that you and others deserve equal consideration, says Gupta. This is also the guiding principle of fairness. Even if you happen to be in a position where you can take undue and unfair advantage over others, you do not if you are fair and ethical. This principle is captured very memorably in the biblical saying, 'Do unto others what you would like them to do unto you.'

In a sense, this is a revolutionary injunction because this appears to go against our instincts. Our instincts, which we share with the rest of the animal world, are self-centred. They are focused on self-preservation and self-promotion: 'I must survive and thrive; I don't care what happens to the rest of the world.' You can see a display of this aggressive self-interest in operation if you throw a few grains into your garden when birds are around. The strongest and the fastest will come and gobble them up leaving nothing for the others. They may drive the weaker ones away if they try to approach the grains. The old and infirm birds will have to be content with what is left over after the powerful birds feast. If they starve and die, it's their problem.

We have, however, learned over tens of thousands of years that queuing up serves our interests better than scrambling, at least in the long term. There is delay but certainty about the result when you queue up. You may be powerful today, but tomorrow you will be old and weak. Or someone more powerful than you may emerge right in front of your eyes and bash you up.

You live in an interdependent world. If you pursue your self-interest too aggressively, that is, without any concern for others' needs and interests, you may have short-term gains but heavy long-term losses. So it is good for the tribe to have some system which ensures fair treatment to everyone irrespective of their current strengths or weaknesses. That system consists of laws, big and small. It assumes that all individuals have equal rights irrespective of the unequal distribution of talent, strength, and wealth. The community supports the rule of law with its collective strength and penalizes those who flout its laws. But there are limits to what laws can define no matter how detailed they are. There are equally severe limits to the enforcement of laws, both domestic and international. Many people violate them for unfair, selfish gains in situations where they believe they will not be caught either because they are clever enough to destroy incriminating evidence or explain it away, or because they have enough resources to stop others from investigating. The simple reason for such violations is that 'what's-in-it-for-me' still drives human behaviour. Civilization has not removed the fundamental animal instinct for preferring one's own good to the common good; it has only put the pursuit of self-interest on leash, as it were.

This is where ethics comes in. It complements law. It covers your social behaviour that is not covered by the letter of the law but by the spirit of the law, which is fair treatment of everyone. In other words, it prompts you to deal with others in a fair fashion even though it does not define fairness. It will, for example, ask doctors not to prescribe diagnostic tests and procedures whose only purpose is to get a commission from the laboratory that conducts them. Laws are, for all practical purposes, helpless here. The ethical code will state that doctors should not prescribe any tests or procedures that are not necessary for diagnosis, but leave the interpretation of 'necessary' to their judgement.

The world of ethics, however, is murky. Here, everyone carries a measuring tape. Everyone believes that their tape is the standard. They measure everything with it and claim that their measurements are right. The trouble is that the measuring tape is extremely elastic. How much you stretch it—and it can stretch a lot—depends on whether you are measuring yourself and friends, or rivals and others. Here also, the pursuit of self-interest drives your interpretation of ethical norms and your justification for any deviation.

THAT EXPLAINS IT!

During the controversy following the Indian Premier League's (IPL) auctioning of franchises in March, 2010, Sharad Pawar, Chairman of the Board of Cricket Control of India and Union Minister for Agriculture, stated publicly that neither he nor his family was directly or indirectly linked with the IPL. When, however, *The Times of India* revealed on Thursday, June 4, 2010, that the Pawars owned 16.22

While there are some ethical norms that are widely accepted, many norms vary significantly between individuals and communities within a country, and between countries and cultures. That you have to keep the promises you make, even when there is no legally binding proof, appears to be accepted the world over. That people have to treat scientific discoveries as intellectual property of companies or individuals and pay the price they set for its use does not appear to have the same level of universality. Communities that have many discoveries in their bag push for the sanctity of intellectual property as private property; others talk about such discoveries as common treasures of the human race. This again brings us back to the role self-interest plays in formulating legal and ethical norms whose ostensible purpose is to ensure fairness for all.

The human race has travelled tens of thousands of years past the hunter-gatherer stage. But might is still right; the mighty still write the rules. This happens at all levels—home, village, district, province, state, country, and the world. The more powerful countries write laws to give themselves maximum advantage in their dealings with the rest of the world just as the more powerful sections of any community formulate rules that give themselves maximum advantage.

They promote norms of ethics in a similar vein. They present their norms as the right ones that should be adopted by everyone. This leads to hypocrisy all around because basic human nature does not change with skin colour or political ideology. Western countries, for instance, rile against bribing common in many African and Asian countries while they find nothing wrong with companies in their own countries contributing to the campaign funds of political parties and buying influence. 'That could be a distinction without a difference,' says Robert Kennedy in a letter to the editor of *The Economist* (May 29, 2010). There are just laws and unjust laws; there are universal ethical norms and partisan ethical norms promoted by powerful lobbies. Thus, the world of ethics is not a straightforward, black-and-white one.

THE MURKY ETHICS OF BUSINESS

If the world of ethics is murky, the world of business ethics is murkier. It is full of pots calling kettles black. Holders of patents, for example, accuse pirates of stealing intellectual property. Pirates accuse patent holders of unconscionably exploitative pricing using their monopoly. Bigger companies routinely use money in various ways including self-serving sponsored research to get governments and international organizations to frame policies or introduce laws that favour their products and services. Some major makers of vaccines and antiviral drugs for swine flu for example, seem to have been behind the WHO guidelines that created a panic the world over and made many countries spend billions of dollars to stockpile their products, according to a report by Council of Europe and another by *British Medical Journal*, both widely discussed in the media during June 2010.

Some companies take the public's attention away from their main business by throwing a few crumbs at activities that come under the label, 'Corporate Social Responsibility.' American oil giant Chevron Corporation, for example, made a net income of US$4,600 million in the first quarter of 2010 (see www.chevron.com), but in a full-page advertisement in *The Economist* on May 29, 2010, it focused on the US$50 million it disbursed as micro-loans to entrepreneurs over a six-year period, that is, about US$2 million a quarter. Readers not familiar with Chevron would be forgiven if they thought that microfinance was its main business.

Everyone pays lip service to ethical values, but violations are common. Some multinational companies that proudly and loudly announce that they never bribe anyone to get business routinely pay money under the table when they do business in Asian and African countries, but call it expenses for customer education or give it some other politically correct label. The more ethically adventurous companies engage brilliant minds to explain away their gross violations of laws and ethical norms that are detected. The avoidance of ethical values by businesses has become so prevalent down the years and across countries and cultures that there is a general belief that you can't be ethically correct and commercially successful at the same time.

Business ethics is nothing but rules and conventions that give businesses a level-playing field for competing and a fair deal to their customers. Trouble starts when a business does something to get an unfair advantage over its rivals. It could be exploiting privileged information, high market share, deep pockets, connection to policymakers, or just great reputation. Many businesses have been quietly endorsing the saying, 'all is fair in war and love,' and extending it to include what they do: fighting for survival, market share, profits, and glory. Their public posture, however, is that the sole purpose of their existence is to enhance the lives of their customers.

Let's call a spade a spade. All commercial organizations are in the business of making money whatever they put in their vision statement. A pharmaceutical company may, for example, shout from the housetop that they are in the business of saving lives. But they would rather see thousands die than lower the price of their patented drugs or share their intellectual property with others. A toy manufacturer may declare that they are working hard to enrich children's lives, but they may readily use toxic paints to reduce costs and increase profits.

There is nothing wrong with making money. In 1970, Milton Friedman, a future Nobel laureate, said so unequivocally. Quoting from his own *Capitalism and Freedom*, he said that the only social responsibility of business was to 'increase its profits so long as it stays within the rules of the game, which is to say, engages in open and free competition without deception or fraud.' He asked executives to 'make as much money as possible while conforming to the basic rules of the society, both those embodied in law and those embodied in ethical custom.'

Many businesses make money without scrupulously following the two conditions Friedman mentioned: obey the law and adopt ethical norms. These two conditions can be collapsed into one: be fair. But before condemning businesses for unethical or unlawful practices, we should also appreciate the difficult circumstances they operate in. A small company may, for example, be forced to bribe an official to get a quality certification that it does not qualify for under the rules; but some of those rules may have been written to favour big companies rather than to ensure quality. A company may claim to have a quality certificate, which it does not; but perhaps the only reason it does not have the certificate is its refusal to bribe the officials concerned.

Similarly, certain violations of laws and ethical norms may not even be perceived as such if they are widely seen and condoned. Use of unaccounted money in buying and selling property in India is a case in point. Thus, the world of business ethics also is full of ambiguities and hypocrisies.

BEYOND THE PALE OF LAW

J.R.D. Tata (JRD) started Tata Airlines in 1932 with the help of a former Royal Air Force pilot, Neville Vintcent. He was passionate about flying and had a good business plan, but getting the government's permission proved to be next to impossible. This is where Vintcent's intervention helped. Being an Englishman he gained access to and discussed with Lord Willingdon, the Viceroy, and Lady Willingdon the idea of a private, Indian airline company. That helped JRD tremendously.

When he started Tata Airlines, JRD entered into a five-year contract with Vintcent, who left a government job to join him. According to that contract, one third of the profits from the airline company would go to Vintcent. In the first year, the company made a net profit of Rs 60,000; in five years it went up to Rs 600,000

When the contract was up for renewal in 1937, JRD's legal adviser told him that there was no need to retain the terms in the original contract, and that he could renegotiate them with Vintcent, whose role had become less critical. He was, indeed, not legally required to retain the same terms. He could now have run the airline alone if Vintcent left the company unwilling to accept less than one third of the profits. But JRD decided to retain the same terms because he felt he was morally obliged to do so.

Source: R.M. Lala, *Beyond The Last Blue Mountain: A Life of JRD Tata*, 1992 New Delhi: Viking/Penguin, pp. 94–5

N.P. Shah, 'Ethics and Corporate Boards http://www.lawyersclubindia.com/articles/Ethics-and-Corporate-Boards, 2009, -1370.asp (Last accessed by the author on August 28, 2010).

BUSINESS ETHICS, BUSINESS SENSE

As the world of business is replete with violations of ethical norms in its pursuit of profit, John Collins asks in a *Business Horizons* editorial, 'Is business ethics an oxymoron?' (Oxymoron is a Greek term that refers to a combination of two contradictory attributes. Examples: thunderous silence, freezing fire.) He goes on to answer that it is not an oxymoron. Good ethics is good business. This is because, he adds, business is not a zero-sum game. Businesses are dependent on several stakeholders such as shareholders, employees, customers, suppliers, and civil society. Paying exclusive attention to the shareholders and maximizing profits for them while alienating the other stakeholders is not good business. It is certainly not good business in the long term. In fact, shareholders are the first to jump ship when they see signs of trouble. Within a month, for instance, of the BP/Haliburton oil spill of April 20, 2010, in the Gulf of Mexico, both these companies lost about a third of their value because their shareholders started dumping the shares (*The Economist*, June 2, 2010).

Thus, we come back to the idea of enlightened self-interest. It pays to be ethical. Being unethical may help you make quick profits but alienate some important stakeholders and hurt your long-term prospects. If you are running a marathon, if you want to grow, you had better be ethical and build up a reputation for being fair in your dealings with everyone. The value of such a reputation can be readily seen from the way brands and trademarks work. Once you trust a brand to be or to deliver what it promises to, you don't ask questions. You just buy it. Similarly, when a potential customer has to choose between companies, especially for a long-term engagement, the reputation for ethical behaviour may be the deciding factor. Many doors will open to representatives of ethical companies.

Transparency is one of the hallmarks of ethical companies. This has major implications for the way employees perceive their company. If there is transparency, there is an excellent chance that fairness will prevail in decision-making and even unpleasant decisions will, as a result, be accepted by those affected. When a senior executive shrouds his decisions in secrecy, he is withholding information that might make it difficult to sell the decision internally. While there is room for secrecy in matters related to a company's strategic moves, many instances of suppressing information from a company's own employees stem from actions that cannot be totally justified, actions that are driven by nepotism or favouritism rather than merit. The unfairness inherent in such actions is not good for the company's health and growth.

Being ethical will force companies to pass up certain opportunities to make quick profits. That does not mean that ethical companies cannot make money. In fact, as Dipankar Gupta says in *Ethics Incorporated: Top Priority and Bottom Line,* 'it is pointless to boast about being ethical if the company's balance sheet makes for a dismal reading.' Being ethical is adopting a sustainable model of doing business. When a company is ethical— fair to all the stakeholders and transparent in its dealings—it will attract business without misleading anyone and will make money. The way Johnson & Johnson dealt with a crisis (see box, The Fall and Rise of Tylenol) in 1982 is a classic case of an ethically correct decision with heavy short-term losses leading to much greater long-term gains.

THE FALL AND RISE OF TYLENOL

In the last week of September 1982, Johnson & Johnson was faced with an unprecedented challenge. Seven people died in Chicago after taking their bestselling painkiller, Tylenol. Someone had laced the tablets in a few bottles with cyanide.

The deadly tampering occurred after the bottles had been dispatched from J&J's plant. No one knew how many bottles had been affected. Recalling all the bottles would be ideal but suicidal from the business perspective. It would cost about US$100 million, a very large sum in 1982. It would kill Tylenol, which had given the company 17 percent of its net income in 1981. The company would lose its presence in the US$1.2 billion painkiller market, where Tylenol's share was a dominating 37 percent.

Under the leadership of James Burke, the chairman, the company decided to put the consumer's safety first. They voluntarily recalled all the Tylenol bottles from the shelves although there was no precedent of such massive recalls of any pharmaceutical products.

Immediately after the recall, Tylenol's market share dropped to 7 percent from 37 as feared; but within two months it shot up to 30 percent when the company introduced tamperproof bottles. J&J's share price plunged, but it recovered soon and scaled new heights.

That difficult decision was the smartest J&J ever made whether it was driven by ethical considerations or by commercial considerations, or a combination of both. Because it was ethically correct, the decision pitchforked J&J into a league of its own. The story of that recall has been analysed tens of thousands of times in management classrooms across the world as a model for ethically correct decision-making in difficult circumstances.

Source: The figures used in this account have been taken from J. Rehak, 'Tylenol made a hero of Johnson & Johnson: The recall that started them all'. *The New York Times,* March 23, 2002.

ETHICAL PERSUASION

All persuasion is, in a sense, manipulation. You polish your apple and show the buyer the part with no blemishes: you present the advantages of your proposal holding back or at least playing down any disadvantages. You don't tell the whole truth even if you are careful to avoid telling lies. You guide the persuadee, in spite of her resistance, to a predetermined target employing various techniques. Is all persuasion, then, unethical? This is a simple question with no simple, straightforward answers.

Would you be an ethical persuader if you suppressed critical information or presented false information to persuade someone to do something that would benefit him tremendously without giving you any special advantage? Would it be ethical, for example, if you exaggerated the evidence of the link between smoking and cancer to persuade your audience to give up smoking, which you believe is harmful for them and for their families? Would you be ethical if you knowingly used false data to persuade someone to do something that would benefit him greatly and also benefit you? Would you be ethical if you tried to persuade someone quoting false data which you believe to be correct but did not bother to verify? There are no straightforward answers to any of these or similar questions.

Sherry Baker and David L. Martinson (2001) identify five principles of ethical persuasion:

▶ The message should be truthful
▶ The persuader should be authentic
▶ The persuadee should be respected
▶ The persuasive appeal should be equitable
▶ The persuasion should be socially responsible

This is excellent advice, but difficult to follow when you want to judge whether your persuasive attempts are ethical or not. Besides, if the bar is very high, whatever the philosophical justification, people respond by not even trying to jump. Thus, the best becomes the killer of the good. It is not at all surprising that a large number of people consider it impossible to be ethical persuaders, especially in the world of business. We need a simpler measure.

If being ethical is being fair to everyone and giving others the same consideration as we give ourselves, ethical persuasion is built on the same principle: Be fair. In persuasion this is translated into giving the persuadees enough information and time to take a reasonable decision even when you know that making some of that information available to them or giving them additional time to think might result in their rejecting your proposal. But what will qualify as 'enough information and time to take a reasonable decision'? Depending on whether you are the persuader or persuadee, your elastic tape will give you different readings. Let's look at a real-life incident, summarised from an account in Rajiv K. Mishra's *Business Ethics: Code of Conduct for Managers*. It is about the unpleasant experience one of his friends had had.

A senior bank manager booked a holiday abroad with a leading tour operator who had extensively advertised it in national newspapers. The package he bought included return tickets for four members of his family and six nights and seven days in a luxury hotel. The price was surprisingly low but the sales executive, who offered a few additional services, persuaded him to book immediately because it was a special, limited time offer. He gladly paid the whole amount at the time of booking to ensure that he didn't miss this great opportunity.

His first shock came when he was asked to apply for visas. That is when he was told that the tour-package price he paid did not cover visa fees and airport charges. He shelled out an additional Rs 15,000. When he returned from the holiday, he realized that the additional expenses were almost equal to the tour price that he had paid. And the hotels where they stayed did not deserve the label, 'luxury.'

To make the discussion easy, let's call the customer Vikram, the tour operator Disha Travels, and its local manager Sumitra. Let us try to recreate the thoughts that went through the heads of these two, the buyer and the seller.

Vikram feels cheated. He believes he is a victim of deception. He thinks that Disha Travels' advertisement misled him by deliberately hiding essential expenses such as visa fees, airport fees, and taxi fares to and from hotels. On the whole he had to spend twice as much as he had anticipated based on that advertisement. This is well beyond what he could have spared for a family holiday. The entire family will probably have to tighten their belts for several months to make up for this. If he had known the full extent of the expenses involved, he would perhaps not have opted for this foreign holiday. He had never taken a foreign vacation because he knew it was beyond his means. He was attracted to Disha Travels purely because of the low and affordable price they had quoted.

Sumitra, however, asserts that Disha Travels did not hide any information. The company promised Vikram return tickets for four members of his family and stay for six nights and seven days in a luxury hotel. And they delivered exactly that for the price they advertised. They never promised to take care of any other expenses in connection with the holiday abroad. Customers would be naïve to think that tour operators would take care of expenses that are not mentioned in the advertisement. Did Vikram think that he and his family would be able to do their shopping also in Singapore at Disha Travels' expense? It is churlish to complain about the level of luxury at the hotel. Did he expect to stay in a seven-star hotel for the pittance he had paid? He and his family were not put up in a dormitory; they were accommodated in a three-star hotel. In any case, why didn't he ask any questions when booking the holiday? If he had asked about visa fees, airport taxes or any expenses not covered by the tour price, he would have received detailed information on how much he should pay. It is unfair to accuse Disha Travels of hiding information when he didn't ask any questions. Disha Travels would be guilty of unethical persuasion only if they gave false information or made false promises. Disha did not.

Both are right. Both are wrong. Both are aggrieved. Disha Travels did not give him enough information or time to take the right decision, especially when he was planning a holiday abroad with his wife and children for the first time in his life. But then he did not ask Sumitra any questions; he did not tell her he was going abroad for the first time; he just assumed that the price quoted by Disha Travels in their newspaper advertisements would cover everything. He cannot realistically expect the managers of Disha Travels to anticipate all kinds of questions and provide answers to them whether customers ask or not. He should have asked questions about any additional expenses, especially because he was booking a foreign holiday for the first time in his life. They did not give him much time because they know that many people don't take a decision unless there is some pressure; Disha Travels needed to fill the seats as soon as possible.

It is obvious that we cannot arrive at clear-cut rules about ethical persuasion. If we draw them up, we may be tempted to obey them in letter rather than in spirit. The best way forward, then, might be to rely on the golden rule: 'Do unto others what you would like them to do unto you.' If you were Sumitra of Disha Travels, you would ask yourself: 'If I were taking a holiday abroad, what kind of information and advice would I like to get from a tour operator?' She should then provide that information, if she wants to be fair to the customer who may not know enough to even ask the right kind of questions. If, based on her experience, she senses that the customer appears to be a first-timer, she should perhaps check if he is aware of additional expenses. She should not look at her job as trapping unwary prospects and picking their pockets legally but as someone helping a partner to enjoy a new experience. Even if he feels he cannot afford a holiday abroad, she may be able to persuade him to buy the holiday if she believes that it is worth tightening one's belt for a few months to get that fabulous foreign holiday experience.

It is amazing to see how creative solutions to apparently intractable problems come up (see box, United We Stand) when you engage your clients as partners rather than as adversaries and discuss things transparently. If you try to trap them into an agreement through fraudulent means, you can expect resentment and, maybe, even sabotage.

UNITED WE STAND

We (the Domestic Appliances and Personal Care Products Division of Philips Electronics India Limited, Pune) had a major problem with Kitchenad Appliances, Mumbai, in 2006. They were our main supplier (about three-fourths) of jar assemblies for our mixer grinders. They wanted an immediate and substantial price hike. If we didn't raise the price, they said they would withhold supplies.

Their demand was largely reasonable. Steel prices were shooting through the roof. But our competition was so tough that we couldn't afford to raise the price of our mixers to offset any extra payments to the supplier. Although we had the benefit of a well known and well trusted brand, price was an important consideration for the middle-class buyers of our mixer grinders.

I was Deputy Manager, Purchase. The management had made it

clear to me that we should not raise the purchase price of any supplies.

I invited Mr Praveen Shah, Owner of Kitchenad, to a meeting at my office in Pune. We talked about our long association since 1998. We talked of the various instances in the past when we worked together to come out of various crises involving large rejections and delayed deliveries. I explained to him the tough situation we were in. I also told him what would happen if we paid him more and raised the price of the mixer to make up for it. Our sales would come down significantly and naturally our off-take from him would come down too.

I suggested that we help him bring down his process costs so that he can maintain his profit margins without raising his prices. I reminded him that being associated with Philips would pay him rich dividends as it had in the past. I also told him that stopping supplies would hardly be the kind of behaviour expected of a partner with whom we shared a decade-old, mutually beneficial relationship.

We ended the meeting with an agreement both of us liked. He promised not to raise the prices under the present circumstances but to ensure uninterrupted supply of jars. He accepted my offer to send our Engineering Manager to his factory to study his processes in depth and suggest ways of reducing cycle time, improving quality, and bringing rejections down significantly.

Source: An account by Ujjal Gupta, Deputy Manager—Purchase & VD, Philips Electronics India Limited, Pune (2006).

Naturally, the extent and depth of information you provide will vary depending on your judgement. If you hold a position where the persuadee does not have the ability to analyse information adequately and trusts you almost blindly, you have to be extra scrupulous. If, for example, you are a surgeon and your persuadee is a patient, it may be unethical for you to present surgery as the only option when alternatives are available. We have used 'may be' rather than 'will be' in the sentence above, because ultimately you should decide whether what you are doing is ethical or not. You may be recommending surgery because, irrespective of what others think and published codes of ethics state, in *your* judgement, surgery is the only realistic option for that particular patient considering his age, occupation, and income; it may be beyond him to analyse all the options adequately and choose one of them. Of course, you could be wrong in your judgement; but that doesn't make you unethical. Asking him to undergo surgery will become unethical only if you believe that surgery is not the best option for him and yet recommend it to him because you stand to get a hefty fee.

In 'The Age of Deception' (*Outlook*, March 20, 2006) Payal Kapadia talks about some victims of Botox treatment. One of them was a 65-year-old housewife, Shanti Modi. The treatment left her lips paralysed. She initially consulted a dermatologist to get the crow's feet around her eyes treated with Botox. According to Kapadia, the doctor should not have initiated the treatment because she was too old for it, but he did. When she returned a fortnight later for a touch up, the doctor persuaded her to have her laugh lines treated too. She paid Rs 30,000 for the treatment, and had paralysed lips to show for it. This appears to be a clear case of unethical persuasion by the doctor. If, however, he had performed the procedure after warning her of the possible consequences, we cannot say that he had persuaded her unethically. No one will know what exactly transpired between the two.

The upshot is that there cannot be clear and unambiguous guidelines when it comes to ethical persuasion. Omission of some information, which you may be able to explain away as an unintentional lapse, can be far more deceptive, destructive, and unethical than providing false information in certain cases. Therefore, it is best to depend on your conscience, with all its haziness, rather than on clarity of definitions. Of course, you should constantly guard against stretching your elastic measuring tape too much.

PERSONAL CODE VERSUS COMPANY CODE

As a company consists of many individuals, how can it become ethical unless everyone is ethical? Is it feasible when the company is very large? An ethical company is one which has created a culture that enables individuals to follow the company's ethical code of conduct and their own principles, which may be even more stringent than that of the company. The company's leaders should set an example by preferring ethics to expedience when they are faced with choices. They should develop a code of ethics that embodies the values they uphold, and make it available throughout the company. Such a code, however, should serve only as a reference point.

The leaders have to nurture a culture of ethics in the company by communicating their values to all the members of the organization through real and truthful stories of how they actually deal with ethical challenges. If a company depends on a code of ethics rather than stories of relevant decision-making at different levels, managers may violate ethical norms and hide behind the letter of the code. The way former US President Bill Clinton justified his statement ('I did not have sexual relations with that woman, Ms Lewinsky.') when confronted with evidence about his inappropriate behaviour with the White House intern Monica Lewinsky is well-known. His fig leaf was his peculiar interpretation of the word, sex. He may have saved his skin, but his reputation was tarnished forever.

True stories of ethical behaviour under testing circumstances are far more powerful than manuals of ethics with detailed dos and don'ts in conveying the nuances of what it means to be ethical. While a detailed statement carries the letter of a company's ethical norms, stories carry their spirit. Stories can educate and inspire everyone in the organization. They also reconfirm the company's continued commitment to those values.

During a public lecture delivered at the Indian Institute of Management, Ahmedabad, a few years ago, the then CEO of Hindustan Lever Ltd (HLL), M.S. Banga, narrated the following incident.

> HLL was getting ready to inaugurate its spacious new corporate office in a big Indian city. All arrangements had been made and invitations to the inauguration sent out. That is when an official from the planning division of the municipal corporation brought to their notice a minor deviation from their new building's approved plan. There was a small addition. No one at HLL had noticed it. The official said that the extra bit had to be removed before he could give them permission to occupy the building. As it was not feasible to do so before the inauguration, the HLL management asked him if they could pay a penalty and get the deviation condoned. He flatly refused. They must remove the extra bit. He, however, showed them a way out. If they paid him Rs 200,000, he would ignore the deviation and get the building approved for occupation. Removing the extra space from the building would cost the company several times that amount and thoroughly upset its schedule. But the top management decided to do that and delay the inauguration by a few weeks rather than pay a bribe. (Note: There may be some minor inaccuracies in this story as this has been recalled from memory.)

This story gave employees of HLL a clearer understanding of the company's policy towards bribing than any circular from the headquarters could have done.

The way Infosys dealt with Phaneesh Murthy, its US-based director of global sales and marketing and member of the board in 2001–2, when a former employee filed a serious sexual harassment case against him in a California court, is well known. (You can find a brief but comprehensive account at Dataquest, http://dqindia.ciol.com/ .) Although Phaneesh Murthy was among the company's most valuable managers because of his pivotal role in strengthening and expanding its operations in the US and although he vehemently protested his innocence in public, he was asked to leave once the rest of the board was convinced that there was sufficient ground for the accusation. While there may also have been pressing commercial considerations behind the decision because of the company's liability in such matters, the move sent out two strong messages. First, the company will not tolerate sexual harassment no matter how high or valuable the harasser and how low the victim. Second, employees will get a fair chance to prove their innocence, if they are falsely accused. Both of these messages continue to comfort the employees and encourage others to either join Infosys or do business with it.

When such accounts of difficult ethical choices made by their leaders go round in a company, all employees get the core meaning of the company's ethical values in a graphic and unmistakable fashion. They serve as models and encourage employees to put values ahead of expedience even when it means loss of revenue and loss of reputation. They are far more persuasive than lists of dos and don'ts accompanied by lists of penalties for violation.

Unfortunately, the stories that go round in many companies are not in alignment with the code of ethics they have formally adopted or the laws of the land they are required to obey. Those stories also indicate to everyone what kind of people will get ahead in the company. Your personal code of ethics may not be in alignment with what your company expects you to do. In certain organizations, such as academic institutions, you may be able to maintain your personal code of ethics without any reference to the organization as a whole or to fellow employees. But in commercial organizations, where you have to constantly act on behalf of the company, you may find yourself unable to ignore or act against the prevalent culture. In such cases, you may have to leave rather than go against your personal code of ethics.

> 'The most important persuasion tool you have in your entire arsenal is integrity.'
>
> —Zig Zigler
>
> 'To be persuasive we must be believable; to be believable we must be credible; to be credible we must be truthful.'
>
> —Edward R. Murrow

Ethical behaviour requires courage, one of the most important leadership qualities. What stops most people from resisting the temptation to resort to unethical behaviour is fear that they may lose out. There is, indeed, a heavy price to be paid for upholding your ethical values, especially when they are in conflict with those of your organization. But it may be an excellent investment in your reputation as a person of principles. Occasionally, a reputation for incorruptibility itself will protect you from attempts by others to influence you unethically—they know it is pointless. There is always demand for people who are trustworthy and value-driven. You must build up your personal credibility and reliability through repeated ethical behaviour.

CONCLUSION

In this chapter, we have defined ethics as the set of rules and norms that govern our behaviour towards others. We have noted that fairness—giving others the same consideration as we give ourselves—is the basis of ethical behaviour in general and in business. Ethical persuasion is guided by the same principle. A manager who tries to sell a product, service, or idea should give the persuadees sufficient information for them to take a reasonable decision on whether to buy it or not. The definition of sufficient will vary significantly depending on the persuader, the persuadee, the context, and the objective. Therefore, the world of business ethics and ethical persuasion will always be full of ambiguities and uncertainties. Ultimately we need to have a personal code of ethics to fall back upon.

LESSONS LEARNT

▶ The basis of ethics is fairness towards everyone including one's own self.
▶ Ethics does not work against promotion of self-interest but sublimates it. So it pays to be ethical.
▶ The world of ethics is full of ambiguities and uncertainties with competing norms.
▶ You have to be an ethical persuader if you want long-term success.
▶ Transparency is a critical component of ethical persuasion.
▶ How forthcoming the persuader should be with information depends on various factors. The decision should be based on a sense of fairness towards the persuadee.

▶ While it is good for companies to adopt a written code of ethics, the ethical values the leaders stand for are best communicated to everyone through real stories of how they deal with ethical choices.

While we argue for ethical persuasion, we realize that there are plenty of people who use deception and fraud. While we strive to be ethical in our persuasion, we should also guard against falling prey to unethical persuasion. We shall turn to that in the next chapter and explore how to resist unwanted persuasion.

REFERENCES

Baker, Sherry and David L. M. (2001). 'The TARES Test: Five Principles for Ethical Persuasion'. *Journal of Mass Media Ethics*, 16 (2), DOI: 10.1207/ S15327728JMME1602&3_6, pp. 148–75.

Collins, John W. (1994). 'Is Business Ethics an Oxymoron?' *Business Horizons*, 37(5), pp. 1-8.

Friedman, M. (1970). 'The Social Responsibility of Business is to Increase its Profits'. *The New York Times Magazine*, September.

Gupta, D. (2006). *Ethics Incorporated: Top Priority and Bottom Line*. New Delhi: Sage.

Mishra, R.K. (2006). *Business Ethics: Code of Conduct for Managers*. New Delhi: Rupa.

10

The Resistant Persuadee

INTRODUCTION

We have been exploring ways of becoming persuasive in our multiple roles, especially as boss, subordinate, peer, and vendor. We have been presenting persuasion as the best means of managing the people we have to work with and getting them to do what we want. Now let us explore how to *resist* persuasion.

If we expect others to be persuaded to do what we want, is it fair to hold out when they try to persuade us? Surely, that is a double standard? Certainly not. It is good to be persuaded. We are persuaded to buy a product, service, or idea when others do their homework for us and show us how it will benefit us. That is when we give up any natural resistance or hesitation we may have and accept their proposal. There is no virtue in being mulish and clinging to an unreasonable position resisting others' attempts to take us on board. Why then should we learn how to resist persuasion?

There are three good reasons why we should learn how to resist persuasion:

▶ Some people might try to persuade us fraudulently. We should not willingly dig our own graves for them to bury us alive. Some might trick us into doing what we may not want to do.

They may not harm us, but we feel foolish when we look back at what we have done. *We need to learn how to identify deceptive persuasion of different shades and protect ourselves against it.*

▶ There are times when we end up doing many things against our will because we are overwhelmed by the persuader's position and power. We say yes without evaluating what they ask us to do. This goes on because we don't resist. We are at fault if we allow others to walk all over us.

▶ Understanding how to resist persuasion helps us deal with others when they hold out, at times highly unreasonably, against our legitimate attempts to persuade them. When we encounter resistance, we may be able to change the way we persuade others if we know what causes it and how it can be softened.

THE WORLD OF FRAUD

In an editorial ('An Intolerable Fraud', February 8, 2008), *The New York Times* commented on Roger Chapin, the 'non-profit entrepreneur' whose charities 'Coalition to Salute America's Heroes' and 'Help Hospitalized Veterans' raised US$168 million from the American public between 2004 and 2006. His appeal for donations reached homes by post. The envelope would typically display the photo of a disabled young soldier using crutches to stand on his only leg. It was accompanied by the appeal, 'Thousands of severely wounded troops are suffering. Will you help them...?' Tens of thousands of Americans readily donated small and not-so-small sums of money thinking that this was the least they could do to reduce the suffering of the brave soldiers who lost their limbs fighting on their behalf.

The donors did not know that three-fourths of the money collected would be spent on 'administrative expenses' of the two charities including seven-figure salaries for Chapin and his wife, their meals, travel, entertainment, and premium golf-club membership. As a well-run American charity spends less than one-third of its collection on administrative expenses, Roger Chapin committed 'an intolerable fraud' on the public, notes *The New York Times*, although he did not violate any laws.

The problem was with the donors. They didn't try to find out where their money went. The moment they noticed that the appeal came from a not-for-profit organization helping disabled veterans, they didn't ask any questions. They wrote out cheques moved by the complex emotions of guilt and generosity. They were easily—far too easily—persuaded to part with their money. Most of them would have been on their guard if it was a for-profit company raising money for disabled veterans. The simple label 'Charity' gave credibility to the two outfits created mainly to benefit the promoters.

This is not at all an isolated case of fraud perpetrated publicly on a large number of people over a fairly long period. We can recall examples of some scam or another that we ourselves or someone close to us were victims of. The advance-fee-fraud, also called the Nigerian scam, has been around for at least four decades luring new victims every year. Newspapers all over the world regularly publish stories of people being duped in different ways. Some of them are local stories, some national, and others international. Victims range from children and illiterate people to brilliant, highly educated professionals. Those who read about scams are amazed at how even intelligent and educated people are talked into the trap. But fraud can hit anyone, including those who think they know all the tricks. That is why it is important for us to understand how and why deception works. Prevention, as they say, is better than cure.

Even if we manage to dodge big swindlers, we may not detect some mild deception we are subjected to until after it is too late. Even if it does not cripple us or our organizations, we should try not to be its victim.

There are four main reasons why we are persuaded too easily by proposals that we should resist:

- ▶ Our tendency to take many decisions at a sub-rational level, which is driven largely by instincts.
- ▶ Our reliance on heuristics or rules of thumb to deal with the complexities of life.
- ▶ Mental laziness that lets us accept without rigorous scrutiny apparently logical but false reasoning.
- ▶ Our overconfidence in our ability to see through deceptive persuasion.

In the following sections, we shall take a close look at each of these reasons.

SUB-RATIONAL DECISION MAKING

We consider ourselves superior to the rest of the animal world because of our rationality. We can go beyond the obvious, the 'here and now.' We can guess, estimate, infer, compare, evaluate and predict. This is at the heart of the cumulative progress of science and technology. While all this is true, there is a sub-rational level where we are no different from animals. Deep-seated instincts and drives rule that world. They help animals look after themselves: eat, beat rivals, find mates, reproduce, and strengthen their species.

The same instincts are so central to us that they operate at the animal level in us, that is, below the radar of reason.

The instincts that help animals look after themselves can also cause their destruction if their enemies figure out what those instincts are and how they work. For example, the instinctive and irresistible attraction animals feel towards food to ensure self-preservation leads them to death traps. A fish that spots a wriggling worm wants to catch it before any rival sees it. It doesn't see the hook inside; it doesn't stop to check where the long string attached to the worm goes. A rat that sees a delicious piece of fresh cassava in a contraption in a field doesn't wonder why that piece is not underground. It goes at the cassava piece, not suspecting that this will be its last meal. The pull towards food is so strong that animals miss many signals that warn them of danger.

We may forgive animals for foolishly walking into such traps; after all they are animals that merely follow their instincts. They cannot beat our guile. Strangely, a lot of our behaviour is no different from theirs in spite of our rational eyes that have an 'x-ray vision.' If someone can stimulate one or more of our drives, they may be able to draw us quietly into a trap without alerting our rationality. They work not only on our basic animal drives for food, sex, and survival, but also on our elevated instincts such as greed, guilt, pride, pity, generosity, inquisitiveness, and the need for recognition, derived from our community-based living.

While we are capable of analysing our actions, evaluating them, and predicting their consequences, we may end up not doing it at all under certain circumstances. Decisions may take place at the sub-rational level dominated by instincts. Or we may ask reason to be a handmaiden to our instincts. Persuaders know this and make use of it. Advertisers try, for example, to present their products or services as great bargains because our greed kicks in and makes us want them, preferably before our rivals can lay their hands on them. If persuaders have fraudulent intentions, they will guide us into the traps they have set by stimulating the most relevant drives. Advance-fee-fraud advertisements, for example, tend to play on human greed. Spies routinely use the lure of sex. Many attempts at mild and harmless deception also work at the sub-rational level.

In *Influence: The Psychology of Persuasion*, Robert Cialdini describes a mother turkey's behaviour towards her chicks. She looks after anything—even a stuffed polecat, her arch enemy—that produces the 'cheep-cheep' sound turkey chicks generally make. The 'cheep-cheep' sound acts as a trigger and leads the mother turkey to a predictable action. Cialdini asserts that we have such triggers too. Most of us will respond with a predictable reaction when such a trigger is pressed. All that a persuader needs to do is to identify the right trigger and press it. He can be reasonably sure how the target will respond.

NEIGHBOUR'S ENVY!

On February 18, 1981, Mrs Dora Wilson looked out of her window in Harlow Newtown and saw a group of men loading her neighbour's priceless Persian carpets into a large truck. 'What are you doing?' she called, knowing her neighbours were on holiday. 'We're taking them to be cleaned, madam,' the workmen replied. Quick as a flash Mrs Wilson decided to take advantage of the service they offered. 'Will you please take mine, too?' she asked. The men obliged. They were burglars.

Source: Frank S. Pepper, *20th-Century Anecdotes*, 1990, London: Sphere Books, p. 121; anecdote originally taken from David Frost, *The World's Worst Decisions*, 1983.

Apart from natural drives, we also have conditioned responses to various stimuli. Behaviourist psychology, which tries to explain human behaviour as a result of stimulus-response conditioning, may be unable to account satisfactorily for intelligence and free will, as cognitivists rightly point out. But it does explain a large part of human behaviour exceedingly well. Ivan Pavlov, the Russian psychologist, proved that conditioning would make a dog salivate at the mere ringing of a bell. Behaviourist psychologists such as B.F. Skinner show that a large part of our behaviour is similarly conditioned. The mind just goes to sleep.

Persuaders know that they can get specific responses from their targets by manipulating the corresponding stimuli. It is not at all a coincidence that in commercials that promote health-related products, ranging from toothpastes to food supplements, the presenter nearly always appears in a doctor's uniform. It is not claimed that they are doctors but the commercials play on our immediate association between doctors and their white uniforms. The advertisers hope that we will treat the actor's words like advice from a trusted doctor. If someone asks us whether they are doctors, most of us will, of course, say they are not, but at the subconscious level, they are doctors. Similarly, a sports icon who appears in a television commercial and tells us 'Glag is the secret of my success,' is an actor paid to mouth the words the advertiser gives him. But we see a sportsperson sharing with us the secret of his own fantastic success and reach out for a bottle of Glag.

EASY RELIANCE ON HEURISTICS

We can characterise some automatic, unthinking behaviour as heuristics in operation. These are rules of thumb or stereotypes that we develop based on our necessarily limited experiences and cultural expectations. They help us deal with the complex world around us. Here are some examples from different fields of human experience.

- Ayurveda is slow but safe.
- If we buy something at a discount sale, we save money.
- The higher the price-tag of a product or service, the better its quality.
- A branded product is better and safer than its unbranded counterparts.
- If a lot of people are buying and using a product, it must be good.
- Newer is better.
- Priests are men of God; you can trust them.
- Expensive deodorants make men attractive to women.
- Strangers are more objective than friends and relations.
- People who travel by public transport are people like us— decent, law-abiding citizens.

Rules of thumb are obviously not fully reliable. Some people who travel by public transport, for example, are not genuine passengers. They may be pickpockets or, more dangerously, terrorists. Yet the rule of thumb works so well and so often that you follow it. Life would be intolerable without such shortcuts. If you tend to look at every fellow passenger as potentially dangerous, you may not be able to step out of your home or use public transport. The guards managing security at an airport, however, check every single passenger before letting him or her in because they can't afford to take any chances whatsoever. Perhaps it is the millionth passenger who turns out to be dangerous. That approach is absolutely impractical at railway stations and bus terminals where there are large crowds. There, the authorities follow the heuristic, 'Treat everyone as a harmless passenger unless they display obvious signs of security risk.'

We rely on such heuristics for decision-making because they reduce the load on the conscious mind, and allow it to process other unfamiliar or critical information. A shopper who is keen on good quality may have a rule of thumb which says, 'The higher the price of a product or service, the better its quality.' She automatically picks up the most expensive model or package without studying its specifications meticulously and feels satisfied that she has received the best product or service. She may be right most of the time about quality, even if she doesn't get value for money. She may waste money on the most expensive model because the higher price may be due to features she is not aware of or she does not intend to use.

Successful advertisers know the power of such heuristics and help create a few in their potential customers. Sellers of packaged milk, for example, try to spread the message, 'Pasteurized milk is safe and healthy; raw milk is unsafe.' Sellers of health drinks and food supplements try to popularize the claim, 'Children's growth will be stunted unless their normal food is supplemented with vitamins and minerals.' The targets may not even be aware of some of the rules of thumb they follow. Once such rules are internalized, people automatically avoid perfectly good raw milk and buy pasteurized milk. Young parents pick up health drinks and food supplements at the supermarket instead of trying to give their children a healthy and balanced diet. They persuade themselves. It doesn't occur to them to question the assumptions behind those actions.

Advertisers identify some of the heuristics that we follow and use them to trick us into buying their wares. Seeing that many television viewers are sceptical of products presented and praised by mercenary models, some advertisers show the reaction of *apparently* genuine consumers to their products. Most of the time, however, these are actors posing as genuine customers. There are, of course, advertisements in which responses of authentic customers are presented, such as the views of people coming out of a cinema hall having watched a recently released film. But then the responses of those who don't gush about the film are edited out so that the television viewers see only highly favourable responses. They work on the viewers' conviction that if so many ordinary consumers are happy with the product, it must be good.

When someone identifies our rules of thumb, stereotypes, and biases, and frames their proposal in alignment with them, it is extremely difficult for us to resist it. We don't even feel we are being persuaded. Instead we feel reassured about what we believe. Going along with such a proposal is as easy as swimming downstream—there is no resistance at all. Political, religious, and cult leaders of all colours routinely employ this strategy to persuade their followers to do their bidding.

THE LAZY PROCESSOR

Our weak defences against deceitful persuasion are further compromised by our lazy processing style. We are blessed with an intellect that can critically analyse the reasons presented in support of proposals and accept or reject them based on rigorous principles of logic. Unfortunately, often we don't make it work hard enough. This is especially so when the proposal matches our basic instincts or drives. We allow quite a few false claims or statements to pass through the gateways of our mind without frisking them thoroughly. We shall list just a few.

Accepting hasty or dishonest conclusions

The most common instance of a hasty conclusion is claiming a cause and effect relationship where there is no evidence for anything more than coincidence. Another is claiming that A is caused by B when B is one of several causes of A. A notorious example is the way the addition of the industrial waste fluoride to drinking water supplies and toothpastes was promoted in the US towards the middle of the twentieth century. The claim was that the addition of fluoride would reduce dental cavities by about 65 percent. But as the BBC reporter Christopher Bryson points out in *The Fluoride Deception*, although dental cavities did come down in the US by about 15 percent since the 1940s, a similar reduction was observed during the same period in other countries that did not add fluoride to their water or toothpastes. Bryson speculates that the reduction in dental cavities was due most probably to improved oral hygiene, better nutrition, and availability of antibiotics rather than addition of fluoride. Even if fluoride helped, it was not the only cause.

At times the persuader makes a tall claim without adequate evidence. There may or may not be any intention to cheat. Their position, however, may be of such authority that others accept it uncritically. When UN's Intergovernmental Panel on Climate Change (IPCC) made an alarming claim in a 2007 report that because of global warming Himalayan glaciers would disappear by 2035, it was generally accepted in spite of dissent by some scientists because of the high credibility of the Nobel Prize winning Panel. It was only in 2010 that this claim was seriously questioned. Interestingly, this challenge was due largely because governments found it difficult to take drastic measures to reduce carbon emission.

Never ask a barber if you need a haircut.

—*Robert Levine.*

Trust, but verify.

—*Ronald Regan.*

At times counterevidence is deliberately held back by the persuader. The powerful tobacco industry in the US, for example, is said to have withheld crucial research evidence about the addictive nature of smoking. Pharmaceutical companies are known to hold back or at least play down information about the side-effects of some of the drugs they promote. Most of us take published research findings at face value. We may not bother to check whether the research has been done independently or paid for by organizations that have some commercial stake in it.

GROWTH INDUSTRY

In 2009-10 there was a television campaign by the makers of a health drink. It was built around the claim that hundreds of children who took the company's health drink in a year-long experiment grew twice as much (6 cm) as children who did not (3 cm).

Many parents who couldn't wait to see their children grow into giraffes emptied supermarket shelves of this particular brand. They didn't question such a blatantly untenable claim. Who conducted this research? Where? How did they (if at all they did) create a large control group and a large experimental group of children in such a way that the only difference between the two was the presence or absence of this particular brand of health drink in their diets? Is food the only or even the main cause of growth? As of now, is it possible for any scientist to predict how many centimetres a child will grow in six months or one year? If accurate predictions are not possible, is it valid to attribute growth to a particular input?

As Sucheta Dalal notes in 'Hidden Persuaders,' Ahmedabad-based Consumer Education & Research Centre (CERC) got LG Electronics to withdraw its ads claiming that their Plasma Gold air conditioner (presumably, among all air conditioners) provided the healthiest air to breathe. LG had no proof to back up that claim. Similarly, CERC refused to take at face value Electrolux Kelvinator's claim about how its Plasma refrigerators preserved the nutritive value of the food kept in them for longer periods than other refrigerators. The company had cited the support of 'an extremely credible and reliable independent laboratory.' But CERC discovered that the laboratory belonged to Toshiba, the refrigerator's manufacturer.

Sellers of products, services, and ideas make all kinds of claims. A lazy mind may accept them without questioning and base buying decisions on them.

Overlooking inconsistencies

In 'An Outline of Intellectual Rubbish,' one of his *Unpopular Essays*, philosopher Bertrand Russell talks about nuns who do not remove their bathrobes when taking a bath. Asked why they do so when no one can see them behind closed doors of the bathroom, they point to the all-seeing God. Russell finds it strange that the nuns should consider God capable of seeing through brick walls but not through bathrobes.

Russell needn't have been surprised at the nuns' behaviour. Many people who try to sell us their products, services, or ideas are guilty of inconsistencies and contradictions in their claims. We often don't catch them out because, in order to detect inconsistencies, our mind has to monitor several statements or claims simultaneously and compare them. As that is too much work, we often take one claim or statement at a time and find it acceptable.

To illustrate the way inconsistencies and even contradictions creep in undetected by the persuadee, we need a longish story. As that is not feasible, here is a simple example. It is an excerpt from a recent e-mail sent by a nationally present bank to its high-net-worth customers. The bank is trying to sell a hike in the charges without enhancing any of the services. Perhaps the bank's costs of providing the services have gone up and it must raise the charges. But instead of saying so this is what the bank states:

> Dear customer,
> In our endeavour to serve you better, we have simplified the charge structure in your savings account. The revised charges enable you to have a better understanding of all the charges that are applicable on the various services being provided by the bank. The revised charges as are as detailed below.
> [...]
> Please note that the existing charge structure shall stand applicable for all other services not detailed herein above. The revised charges shall come into effect from...

The first two sentences make a claim about simplifying the charge structure and making it easier to understand. The rest of the e-mail is about all kinds of charges for different kinds of services presented with the accompaniment of many acronyms which are not explained at all. Perhaps the bank expects that the first two sentences will lull the customer so that she does not actually scrutinize the details or take the trouble of comparing them with existing charges.

Accepting Conclusions Built on Inadequate Data

We regularly come across conclusions drawn from surveys of all kinds. As we have seen in Chapter 2, inductive reasoning is a valid form of arriving at conclusions about a whole class based on a study of a part of it. For the conclusions to be tenable, however, the survey has to follow several norms regarding sampling and the kind of questions being asked. But many surveys do not follow the norms of scientific data collection. Sweeping generalizations are made from tiny databases.

Some conductors of surveys deliberately choose biased samples so that they can arrive at the kind of conclusions they want. Some are unaware of the bias in the samples they have chosen. Such defects could seriously damage the validity of the conclusions. Accepting conclusions of such surveys without asking how they were conducted is yet another instance of intellectual laziness.

Inability to Separate a Person from his View

Samuel Johnson, the eighteenth-century English author and lexicographer memorably observed: 'Testimony is like an arrow shot from a long bow; the force of it depends on the strength of the hand that draws it. Argument is like an arrow shot from a crossbow, which has equal force though shot by a child.' We do attach a lot of importance to who says what. If the speaker has credibility, we accept it. If the speaker does not, we reject it. This is why we have been arguing that we must develop our credibility if we want to be persuasive.

There is, however, another side. We have to learn to separate the idea from the speaker. We may be tempted to accept certain things blindly because they come from sources that are supposed to be credible or powerful. And we may reject things blindly because they come from sources we don't approve of or don't care about. Both these are signs of a lazy mind. We should definitely give weight to the source, but not in a blind or automatic manner. The simple reason is that there have been many instances of highly regarded individuals and institutions proving unworthy of the trust placed in them. We have already referred to the way WHO made a pandemic mountain out of a swine-flu molehill. One of the major reasons for the international financial crisis of 2007–8 is the blind acceptance by investors of the ratings of companies and securities by the two highly regarded and powerful international rating agencies, Moody's and Standard & Poor's, as Kathleen Casey and Frank Partnoy observe in The New York Times article 'Downgrade the Ratings Agencies' (June 4, 2010).

All over the world, there are many brilliant scientists and well-established research institutions whose recommendations need to be scrutinized thoroughly before they are accepted because they might be singing someone else's tune. The funding they receive from the government or corporate sector might make them suppress critical information or dilute serious problems. It is not always easy to find out if the conclusions are tainted, and it may not matter if you are not going to take any serious decisions based on that. If, however, such conclusions form the basis of a major move in your life, you had better not go blindly by the researchers' or research institutions' reputation.

More Traps

At times people use language dishonestly but leave a loophole to escape through if confronted. Thus, a tiny asterisk attached to a bold and alluring promise may take us to virtually illegible conditions in small print that negate almost everything in the promise. Or they may appeal to irrelevant issues and take our attention away from the real issue. They may even discuss an irrelevant issue in great detail, settle it, and then claim that as a result the original issue has been settled. We have to watch out for such red herring. Another way in which we are similarly fooled, if we are not careful, is when A shoots down his interpretation of B's idea, and claims that therefore B's idea has been discredited. A's interpretation could be plain wrong! See, for example, the argument in the box below (Give a Dog a Bad Name and Shoot It). In the first paragraph the writers interpret the government's insistence on successful track record for those who bid for public private partnership in the construction of airports as caused by the difficulty in clearly specifying 'output service level requirements.' In the second paragraph the writers claim that there are two inherent flaws in the government's reasoning. However, it is easy to see that the flaws are not in the government's reasoning but in their interpretation of it.

GIVE A DOG A BAD NAME AND SHOOT IT!

After making a case for a Model Concession Agreement (MCA) for Public Private Partnership (PPP) in airport construction like the MCA in road construction, the writers critique the bidding process currently adopted by the government:

Technical bid specifications: In the case of roads, output service level requirements can be easily translated into technical specifications regarding lane width and the like. Moreover, there is uniformity in the requirements for different roads in terms of these basic quality standards. Such clear terms cannot be laid down for airports which vary widely in their passenger traffic and size. Therefore, the current system requires all potential bidders to have had a minimum of five years of experience in the construction industry to be deemed technically competent (Ministry of Finance, December 2007). They are also expected to have a track record of profitable projects in recent years. This condition is viewed as a proxy for the output service level, the belief being that a hitherto successful company will continue to deliver good results in future as well.

However, we believe that such reasoning has two inherent flaws. The first is the problem of the moral hazard involved in selection. Once a contract has been awarded to any one party, it enjoys a monopoly power (especially in the case of airports) over the delivery of services. As a result, there is no incentive for it to maintain its past level of service. Therefore, the track record of a company in the past is no guarantee of its performance in the future. Secondly, such an approach encourages the automatic favouring of a few players over all others. Under the present system, once a player can claim to have been awarded one project on the strength of its credentials, it automatically lays a much stronger claim on all subsequent projects that it bids for. This makes it extremely difficult for a technically sound but new entrant to successfully bid for a project. Moreover, over time, such a system can foster the growth of close relations between the consistently successful player and government officials. Such relations are unhealthy and have the potential to destroy the free and open nature of the selection process.

Source: Taken from *M.M. Monippally Academic Writing: A Guide for Management Students and Researchers*, 2010. An MBA student report (2009), 'Public Private Partnership for Bridging the Infrastructure Gap in India: Airports'. New Delhi: Sage, pp. 126–7.

Other fallacious arguments include statements like the following:

- ▶ It's okay because everyone is doing it.
- ▶ The 500,000 people who elected me are not fools; neither am I.
- ▶ Product X is absolutely safe because no one has conclusively proved that it is unsafe.
- ▶ Baby skin is soft, therefore, it needs our baby oil.

If we analyse these and similar statements, we can easily see that the reasoning is not valid. The makers of such statements get away with them because we are too lazy to analyse them critically. They do not always intend to deceive; they may genuinely believe in those claims and statements. That does not absolve us of our responsibility to process them carefully and critically.

THE GOLIATH COMPLEX

According to the Book of Samuel in the Bible, Goliath was a giant. He was the champion of the Philistines who were fighting Israelites at the Valley of Elah during the reign of King Saul. For forty days he challenged the Israelites to send up someone who would fight him. They dared not respond to his challenge. No one was willing to confront this strong 9-footer in armour. That is when David, a shepherd in his teens, entered the scene quite by chance. He had no armour. He had a shepherd's staff, a sling, and a pouch of pebbles.

Goliath mocked at the puny champion sent up by the Israelites. But before he could figure out what was happening, David took out his sling, took aim, and shot a small pebble. It hit the giant's forehead, and brought him down. David ran up to him, drew out the giant's sword, and cut off his head.

We feel and act like Goliath when we look at the army of persuaders around us. If we are educated or if we hold a high position, we are particularly prone to considering ourselves beyond the reach of their silly tricks. We believe that if we agree to do something, it is because we have considered it critically and have decided to do it. There is no way anyone can dupe us into doing it. We are too smart and too knowledgeable to be taken for a ride.

Such overconfidence in our ability to see through deceptive persuasion strategies is perhaps our biggest weakness. We may realize too late that there were chinks in our armour and that we were far more vulnerable then we had imagined ourselves to be.

There are examples galore of highly intelligent and knowledgeable people falling easy prey to mere slingshots. A well known case is that of Manubhai Shah, who founded the Consumer Education Research Centre (CERC) in Ahmedabad and was its chairman for over twenty years. He fought and won many cases in favour of consumers. His name was the most formidable in consumer activism in Gujarat during those years. Then, around 2006, he 'fell head-long into a Nigerian estate deal that smacks of a scam,' says Radha Sharma ('Consumer Activist Fights to Clear Name,' *The Times of India*, November 23, 2006). He was so sure that he could catch any tiger by its tail, he paid a con artist a total of Rs 4.5 million to get hold of one Justine Collins' unclaimed fortune in Nigeria. When the story broke, he was still hopeful of laying his hands on that Nigerian property. It was impossible for him to believe that he, of all people, was outwitted by some swindlers.

Psychology professor Dr Robert Levine opens his book, *The Power of Persuasion* by narrating how he was taken for a ride by Mario, a lowly chimney sweep whom he had met a few days earlier at a children's soccer game. Mario's first move was to disarm the professor by charging a few dollars less than what they had settled in advance for cleaning the chimney. He said he felt he should reduce his charges because the job took less time and effort than he had expected. Honest-to-the-bone Mario! Before leaving the premises, however, he managed to sell the learned professor two bottles of some useless solution for the 'discounted' price of US$250.

We don't know if the story is true or made up to illustrate a point. It doesn't matter. It is perfectly credible. 'One of life's cruel ironies is,' says Levine, 'that we're most vulnerable at those very moments when we feel in least danger. Unfortunately, the illusion of invulnerability pretty well defines our resting state.' He goes on to cite various research studies which indicate that the vast majority of people consider themselves above average and above being manipulated. A clever con artist who has decided to strike us first makes us feel that it is impossible for anyone to fool us. That lulls us into a sense of security. We are so impressed by our heavily fortified front door that we fail to notice that our back door is open.

Our belief in our immunity to the persuasion bug manifests itself in many ways. One of them is the conviction many of us have that we are not influenced by advertisements. We readily concede that others—the masses—are influenced. But not us. We take rational decisions based on our analysis of the pros and cons of a course of action. We know all about the persuasion tricks in the advertisers' bag. As Dr Robert Levine notes, we firmly believe that we are immune to the charms of advertisements. We are highly mistaken.

Indeed we are fully armed and we expect our opponent to appear in armour. We're prepared for every single move that he is supposed to make. We snigger when a shepherd boy strolls in with just a sling. We, however, fall as we try to laugh him off the court.

BUILDING IMMUNITY

The first step towards building immunity is to accept that we can never achieve absolute immunity. When we replace hubris with humility, we hold a better chance of detecting attempts at deceptive persuasion. Then we will not assume that the backdoor is locked. Rather, we will get up from the comfortable couch in the sitting room, go to the kitchen, and check whether the back door is locked or not. On certain occasions, we may discover, to our horror, that the backdoor is indeed open although we thought we had locked it.

We have seen earlier in the chapter that we fall prey to fraudulent persuasion mainly because we take quick decisions without making our critical faculty work hard. There is a very good reason for it. We have to get on with our lives. We will not get very far if we stop at each step, examine the ground thoroughly, verify that it is safe, and then take the next step. It is neither feasible nor necessary unless we are walking through a minefield.

We, then, have to make a distinction between simple instances of everyday persuasion attempts and the more serious ones leading to major decisions with significant consequences for ourselves or our organizations. When faced with simple persuasion attempts, we can follow the heuristics we have built on our experiences and determined by our values. We can trust our instincts, and take many decisions at the sub-rational level. We can accept certain arguments even if they do not stand critical scrutiny. The simple reason is that often it doesn't matter whether we crack open the small end or the big end of the hard-boiled egg that we want to eat. Whatever the virtues passionately claimed by followers for either end, as Jonathan Swift delightfully described in his *Gulliver's Travels*, we know that it makes no difference either to the nutritional or aesthetic value of the egg. We can go along with what others are doing or ask us to do. There is little virtue in resisting it.

We may hate to admit it but some of our heuristics are fathered by repeated social, religious, and commercial advertisements targeted at us through multiple channels. And some of the scientifically baseless claims made by persuaders of all hues do work in mysterious ways. Take, for example, the ridiculous claims made in television commercials on behalf of men's deodorants: If you wear them, young women in your vicinity will chase you because you will turn them on. Certain experiments show (see box, The Magical Deodorant) that deodorants do enhance men's sex appeal, but not for the reasons the advertisers give. The deodorants work simply because the men firmly believe that they will work.

THE MAGICAL DEODORANT

In an experiment conducted by Dr Craig Roberts of the University of Liverpool and his colleagues it was found that men improved their self-confidence when they used deodorants. The more surprising finding was that the improvement in self-confidence was so high that women who watched them found them attractive even when those women didn't smell the fragrance or know that the men were wearing one. Those men's sex appeal lay not in their looks or in the fragrance of the deodorant they were wearing but in their self-confidence that was signalled by the way they were sitting, walking, and generally holding themselves.

Source: Based on the article, 'The Scent of a Man,' *The Economist,* (December 20, 2008).

When we respond to everyday persuasion attempts without straining our intellects, we will occasionally find ourselves duped. Little harm is done. Rather, we learn a lesson. When we are stung, we add one more rule to our book of heuristics.

Persuasion attempts leading to major personal or professional decisions have to be taken entirely differently. Here the stakes are high. Here we have to keep our antennae up. Our instincts and heuristics will play a role, but we need to engage our mind seriously to make sure that we don't fall prey to fraudulent persuasion. We have to be sceptical, especially when the proposal appears to be very attractive or exclusive. Extreme secrecy should also arouse our critical antennae. It is a good idea to consult someone whose judgement we trust. They may be able to process the same information differently and give us valuable advice that may go against our instincts or heuristics. In such cases avoiding a spot decision is virtually essential. Delaying a decision or consulting a colleague may clash with our conviction that we are above being manipulated. But this is precisely where we need to get rid of our Goliath Complex and recognize that we are vulnerable.

Our understanding of how persuasion works comes to our rescue here. If we know what persuasive moves or techniques we need to make in order to persuade others, we should expect others to know them too. As we noted above, there is nothing wrong with being persuaded. What we need to prevent is being tricked into doing things that we don't want or being persuaded fraudulently. Our awareness of the process of persuasion will help us not only to analyse the approach our persuaders are following, but also ask them searching questions to bring out in the open information that they may be holding back or glossing over.

Some heuristics also alert us to potential deception. A fairly reliable rule of thumb in this context is, 'If something is too good to be true, it is not true.' In fact, barring a few truly exceptional cases, if something is too good to be true, it is likely to be illegal also. Another useful rule of thumb is, 'If someone is pressing you for a quick decision, delay it.' Of course, there is a risk that you will miss a great opportunity if you don't act immediately. Occasionally, you will miss a great opportunity to own something or to make money. But it is more likely that you will avoid a trap that is waiting for you.

RESISTING ASSERTIVELY

In B.K. Karanjia's biography of Ardeshir Godrej, *Vijitatma: Founder-Pioneer Ardeshir Godrej*, there is an account of an encounter the young entrepreneur had with the British proprietor of a shop that sold surgical instruments. He had made some fine surgical instruments and wanted them to be sold through the Englishman's shops. He showed them to the proprietor, who was impressed by their quality and was eager to sell them as imported instruments. Ardershir said they should be advertised and sold as Made in India, because that is what they were and he was proud of their being Indian. The Englishman disagreed because he was convinced that even Indian surgeons, accustomed exclusively to imported instruments, would not touch surgical instruments made in India.

After some argument Ardershir made it amply clear that he would not allow anyone to sell his instruments unless they were presented as made in India. The Englishman observed that the young man was throwing away a great opportunity to make a lot of money. Young Ardershir walked out of the deal.

The Englishman was right about the market. It was not ready to buy Indian-made surgical instruments. What is remarkable here is young Ardeshir Godrej's self-belief and willingness to take risks in a hostile market. His surgical instruments business failed later. But that did not stop him. He went on to make safes that were superior to European ones, and built an industrial empire.

Many of us don't display even a tenth of Ardeshir's self-esteem and courage to speak one's mind even in conditions that are far more favourable than the ones he encountered. Often, we allow others, especially bosses and peers, to persuade us without facing any resistance whatsoever from us. We are overwhelmed by their position or their power to do us harm. Fearing the consequences of saying no to their requests we do what they ask us to without even evaluating their proposal. After a while they take our compliance for granted. Once our minds' muscles atrophy from lack of exercise, we find it almost impossible to make them work. Surprisingly, those who hold us by the throat are not just our bosses. They could be anyone who can press our fear buttons.

NOT FOR SALE

The poor are bankable. They don't need charity; they need commercial credit. This was the firm belief on which Muhammad Yunus, winner of the 2006 Nobel peace prize, founded and nourished the Grameen Bank in Bangladesh. Therefore he rebuffed many attempts by do-gooders including the World Bank to give him grants in aid and soft loans.

In 1995, the World Bank offered Bangladesh government a soft loan of US$175 million on condition that US$100 million of it would go to Grameen. The finance ministry asked Yunus for his comments. He wrote back saying that Grameen did not need any money from the World Bank. This put the Finance Ministry in a difficult position. They had worked hard on getting this soft loan from the World Bank. The finance secretary, 'a respected long-time acquaintance,' invited Yunus for a discussion.

The finance secretary tried his best to persuade Yunus. He said that Grammen did not need to draw down a single taka; all he wanted was a declaration that Grameen was willing to consider this line of credit. Yunus replied that even if Grameen did not draw down a single taka during the next twenty years, the World Bank would forever treat Grameen as a client, as a recipient of their money.

Then the secretary changed the line of argument. He said Bangladesh needed that money. He asked Yunus to think of the poor before refusing the loan. 'I am thinking of the poor. It is exactly for them that I am taking this seemingly inconsistent position,' replied

Yunus. He reminded the secretary that Grameen was built on the firm conviction that the poor are bankable, that they don't need charity. Accepting aid would destroy everything that he and his colleagues had built up over almost two decades. In fact, Grameen was about 'to break completely free of any aid support.'

Finally Yunus said: 'When I came here today I was worried that I would lose a friend I respect because I would put you in an impossible situation. And I was incredibly agitated and anxious, but I cannot go against my conscience. I cannot repudiate everything Grameen has struggled for.'

The finance secretary shook hands with him and promised not to pressure him anymore.

Commenting on that exchange with the finance secretary, Yunus said: 'I felt like my death sentence had just been lifted!'

Source: Summarised from Muhammad Yunus *Banker to the Poor: The Story of the Grameen Bank.* 2007. New Delhi: Penguin (pp 20–2).

There are two serious problems with our failure to resist others' persuasive attempts in spite of our wanting to. First, we will feel unhappy with ourselves. We can never find happiness by doing what we don't want to do, especially when we realize that we didn't have the courage even to let the others know that we didn't want to do it. We will despise ourselves for being so cowardly, and for not being able to do anything about it. The worst part is that we will ultimately make everyone unhappy because we will discover that we cannot meet everyone's conflicting demands no matter how hard we try and how much we sacrifice.

Second, by not offering resistance—essentially, not speaking our mind—we may contribute to poor decision-making. Some very bad decisions are made at the highest levels in organizations because people are unwilling to stand up to their boss and tell him what they really think of his plans or decisions. In that sense, resistance may be a favour you do your boss or peers and to your organization.

There are no easy solutions for the problem of being non-assertive and non-resistant. All we can say is that it is important to be assertive and to speak our mind when others try to persuade us, pressure us, or blackmail us. Persuaders do not welcome resistance. But resistance is good; it is like the weights we lift to strengthen our muscles. It makes the persuader think harder and arrive at better products, services, and ideas.

CONCLUSION

We have argued that there is nothing shameful about being persuaded provided the persuasion is done right. We can buy a product, service, or idea when others show us how it will benefit us or our organization. Unfortunately, there are many instances of deceptive persuasion ranging from mild and harmless ones to very serious ones, threatening the existence of a whole organization. It is, therefore, important to learn how to detect deception and to resist attempts at deceptive persuasion.

There are also instances of legitimate persuasion where we offer little or no resistance because we are afraid of the consequences of dissent. We end up doing many things or supporting many decisions against our will because we are overwhelmed by the persuader's position and power. We say yes without evaluating what they ask us to do. This weakens governance and leads to poor decision-making in organizations. Therefore, we must learn to speak our mind and resist attempts to persuade us if we believe that the proposal is not worthy of adoption.

We have also noted that analysing our own resistance will help us understand why others resist our legitimate proposals even when presented with transparency. Understanding resistance may help us change the way we persuade others and make it more effective.

Lessons Learned

▶ Fraud is deceptive persuasion; fraudsters cheat us with our willing cooperation.

▶ Fraudsters exploit our sub-rational decision-making, driven largely by instincts. At that level, we behave like animals that are drawn towards death traps by the strong urge for food.

▶ We have triggers and conditioned reflexes; people who figure them out can control our behaviour without our realizing it.

▶ When we rely blindly on heuristics to deal with the complexities of life, we risk being fooled by those who figure out our rules of thumb.

▶ Although we can, we don't often make our minds scrutinize the logical rigour and consistency of the proposals made to us; we accept many logical fallacies.

▶ Our overconfidence in our ability to see through deceptive persuasion is a major weakness that swindlers exploit. They make us feel invulnerable before striking from an angle that we least expect.

▶ The first step towards detecting deceptive persuasion is admitting our vulnerability, irrespective of the level of our education and depth of our experience.

▶ To prevent being taken for a ride, we should develop a healthy, sceptical attitude towards others' proposals, especially when they are unusually attractive.

▶ Reasonable resistance can be a favour we do our bosses, peers and our organization.

- Assertive resistance leads to better decision-making and better governance.
- Understanding resistance to persuasion helps us figure out why others resist our attempts at persuading them and adopt new strategies.

REFERENCES

Bryson, C. (2004). *The Fluoride Deception*. New York: Seven Stories Press.

Casey, K. and Partnoy, F. (June 4, 2010,). 'Downgrade the ratings agencies'. *The New York Times*.

Cialdini, R. B. (1993) *Influence: The Psychology of Persuasion*. New York: Quill William Morrow.

Dalal, S. (August 3, 2006). 'Hidden Persuaders'. Available from http://www.moneylife.in/article/76/781.html.

Karanjia, B. K. (2004). *Vijitatma: Founder-pioneer Ardeshir Godrej*. New Delhi: Viking, Penguin.

Levine, R. (2003). *The Power of Persuasion: How We Are Bought and Sold*. New Jersey: John Wiley.

Parekh, S. (December 17, 2008). 'Satyam – Name and Reputation are Upside Down.' Available from http://blog.livemint.com/initial-private-opinion/?p=163.

Russell, B. (1950). *Unpopular Essays*. New York: Simon & Schuster.

Conclusion

On the eve of the Kurukshetra War, Arjuna is distressed by the thought of having to kill his teacher Drona, grand uncle Bhishma, and many other friends and relations. He decides not to fight and throws down his bow and arrow. Krishna tries many different techniques to persuade him to fight. Arjuna resists all of them. Finally Krishna reveals himself in all his glory, and Arjuna agrees. Once persuaded, he fights to the finish without any hesitation.

The same Krishna tries to persuade righteous Karna to leave the evil Duryodhana and join the Pandavas in their fight against Adharma. He gives solid reasons and reveals previously hidden facts in support. Karna agrees with everything Krishna tells him but refuses to leave Duryodhana. Karna's loyalty to his friend and benefactor is so deep that neither the exciting news that he is not a Sutaputra but Kunti's firstborn nor the incredible opportunity to be the Pandava King and Draupati's husband makes a dent in his determination. Krishna fails in his mission. But there is no bitterness. Krishna embraces Karna and bids him farewell.

There are several lessons in these two stories from the Mahabharata. You may be able to change someone's mind even when the target is formidable and the resistance well founded. And you may fail even when you have all the logic in the world in your support and you make offers that you consider irresistible.

Persuasion is not guaranteed even if you play all the cards right. Yet we should try it because once persuaded well, the target joins your camp. Even if you fail, you fail honourably. If you are the target of persuasion, there is nothing shameful about changing your mind in response to the right argument, but you should resist it if accepting the proposal goes against your core values.

So where do we go from here? If you want to be a successful manager, it is not enough to be a one-trick-monkey. You have to become persuasive in your dealings with your bosses, peers, subordinates, vendors, and customers. If you are successful in any of these relationships without being persuasive, you ought to be concerned. You are perhaps achieving much less than what you are capable of. Or some nasty surprises are waiting in the wings for you.

The objective of this book has been to give you tools and illustrations to review your managerial relationships systematically from the persuasion angle. We looked at ethos, pathos, and logos, the three fundamental persuasion factors. We looked also at the most common persuasive moves:

- ▶ Making oneself likeable
- ▶ Leveraging authority
- ▶ Creating indebtedness
- ▶ Stroking the target's ego
- ▶ Playing on herd instinct
- ▶ Getting small commitments
- ▶ Appealing to shared values
- ▶ Engaging the target in consultation
- ▶ Using inductive and deductive reasoning

Unfortunately, there is no formula that you can apply to choose the right strategy. In fact, there is nothing like 'the right persuasive strategy' independent of the persuader, the persuadee, and the context. You have to identify the moves that you are most comfortable with, and the moves that your targets are most likely to respond to. You will not always manage to persuade your target irrespective of the strategy you use and the beauty of your proposal. You may also come across contexts where it may not be worth your while investing in bringing people on board through persuasion. The decision depends on you.

To make persuasion a way of managing and to become a persuasive manager you need to do two things. First, plan your major persuasion efforts systematically. Identify the contexts where persuasion is the right approach. Analyse the target's position, nature, strengths, and weaknesses. Find out the real source of resistance and estimate its strength so that you can frame your proposal in the most attractive fashion. Analyse your own strengths and weaknesses vis-à-vis the target. Then choose the appropriate combination of techniques or persuasive moves to build up your strategy. Don't assume that you can take your target from point 0 to 10 at one go. It may be a slow journey with several stops, but is worth taking. Be prepared to change your strategy if some of your calculations go wrong. If you realize that someone else may be able to do the job better than you, enlist her services.

Second, review both your successes and failures systematically. This is as important as, may be more important than, planning because some of your most successful moves may be instinctive rather than planned. The systematic review gives you insights into the process of managing people, into what works with you and what works with your targets. If you write down your experiences and compare them, you may discover that there are certain patterns in your successes and failures. Contrary to what experts and successful persuaders swear by, you will find that certain recipes of your own work best for you or with your particular targets. It is an accumulation of these insights that will make you a persuasive manager.

When you review your persuasion efforts, ask yourself whether you followed the golden rule of fairness that you have adopted for your dealings with others. Again, a systematic review will help you identify the kind of contexts where you succumb to the temptation to violate your own rule in your eagerness to sell your products, services, or ideas.

You must also review your experiences of being persuaded. Were you persuaded far too easily? Why? Were you overwhelmed by the persuader? Or by some of your own instincts? Did you allow your mind to go to sleep? What can you do to prevent a recurrence?

In the twin process of systematic planning and reviewing you will find it useful to listen to or read other people's accounts of how they dealt with specific challenges of persuasion. You need not ape anyone but you are bound to get some very useful ideas. A word of caution, however, is in order. Don't take any account too seriously because all 'true' stories are somewhat fictional. Many inconvenient truths will be swept under the carpet and ugly missteps eliminated. Just the opposite may also happen. The challenges faced or mistakes made may be exaggerated to make the account compelling. Many things are not what they appear to be or claim to be.

Here one is reminded of the story of a young man's daring rescue of a billionaire's daughter. She falls overboard into icy waters from a luxury cruise liner where her father is partying with guests. The horrified father appeals to the young men around to save her. No one moves. Everyone stands petrified with their eyes fixed on the struggling, flailing woman. And then, all of a sudden, a brave young man jumps into the water, saves her, and brings her up to the deck. The overwhelmed billionaire offers him anything that he would ask, including, of course, his pretty daughter's hand. The young man, still shivering, replies, 'All I want is to know is who pushed me overboard.' When the billionaire father tells the story, he will not remember this last bit. What he will remember is a young man responding instantly to his appeal and jumping into the water risking his life. The old man wants to demonstrate the power of his appeal. As he repeats the story, there may be several young men jumping into the water in response to his appeal.

It is not as though anyone is deliberately putting out false stories. The narrator's memory often plays tricks as Hillary Clinton, American presidential candidate, discovered in 2008. To convince the electorate that she had the experience and courage to deal with any crisis, she vividly described how she had to run across the tarmac to avoid sniper fire when she, as First Lady, landed in Bosnia in 1996. She soon had to withdraw the story when, as reported by *The New York Times* on March 25, 2008, 'CBS News showed footage of her walking calmly across the tarmac with her daughter, Chelsea, and being greeted by dignitaries and a child.' She said she 'misspoke' about the incident.

Thus you should expect others' accounts of their successes and failures in persuasion to be spiced up. That doesn't stop you from learning a trick or two for your own journey.

Happy journey on the persuasion road!

A note on the author

Professor of communication at Indian Institute of Management Ahmedabad, Mathukutty M Monippally specializes in strategic communication, leadership communication, persuasion, and bad news delivery. He has designed and runs training workshops in different aspects of managerial communication for middle, senior, and top managers of national and multinational companies, especially in IT- ITeS, banking and financial services, pharmaceuticals, and automobiles. He can be reached at mpally@iimahd.ernet.in and www.PersuasiveManager.blogspot.com.

A note on IIMA Business Books

The IIM Ahmedabad Business Books bring key issues in management and business to a general audience. With a wealth of information and illustrations from contemporary Indian businesses, these non-academic and user-friendly books from the faculty of IIM Ahmedabad are essential corporate reading. www.iimabooks.com

Would you like to participate

in the IIMA Guru Yatra?

For more details visit

www.iimabooks.com

Other books in this series

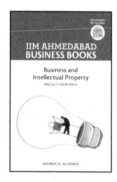

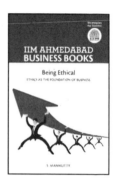

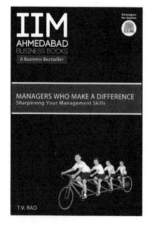

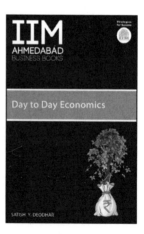